U.S. Nuclear Strategy for the Post–Cold War Era

Glenn C. Buchan

RAND

PREFACE

This monograph examines U.S. options for revising its nuclear strategy and force structure in the post–Cold War era. It evaluates those options in the broader context of overall U.S. security policy in a time of flux when traditional alliances are crumbling, the political map of the world is changing, and weapons of mass destruction are spreading.

The monograph itself is extracted from a forthcoming book on U.S. nuclear strategy in the post–Cold War era. It presents the "prescriptive" part of the analysis, which should be of most interest to policymakers. Accordingly, it omits much of the detailed support for the various conclusions, although it does present the basic lines of reasoning that support all of the major themes. Similarly, it includes only the necessary minimum set of obligatory citations and footnotes.

This research was initiated by the author. The monograph was not prepared in fulfillment of a RAND contract or grant; it is published by RAND, using its own funds. The original version of this monograph was prepared for the Nuclear Policy Review announced by Secretary of Defense Les Aspin in late 1993. Subsequently, Dr. Paul K. Davis, corporate research manager of the Defense and Technology Planning Department at RAND, suggested that the draft be published, believing that it would be of interest to a wider audience. In particular, the monograph should be of interest to planners and policymakers involved with shaping U.S. nuclear policy and structuring U.S. military forces as well as lay audiences with interests in these areas.

CONTENTS

FIGURE AND TABLES

Figure

Tables

SUMMARY

The United States needs to take advantage of the rare opportunity that the end of the Cold War provides to revise its nuclear strategy and force structure to deal with whatever the future might hold. For once, a *confluence of institutional interests might actually permit an effective working consensus* to develop on what nuclear forces can do for the United States, what those nuclear forces ought to look like, and how they should be operated. Even more important, its own *nuclear weapons may no longer be the key to protecting the United States from the range of nuclear threats that could evolve* in the post–Cold War world. U.S. policymakers need to understand both the opportunities and the risks that such a change in direction might pose.

U.S. FOREIGN POLICY IN THE POST–COLD WAR ERA AND THE ROLE OF NUCLEAR WEAPONS

In the post–Cold War world, there should be many fewer situations that demand the use of U.S. military force, and few of those should involve any risk of nuclear confrontation. Indeed, a *primary U.S. policy objective should be to make nuclear weapons less important rather than more important as instruments of policy.* The trick is to encourage nuclear forces to "wither away" while maintaining a nuclear capability that could actually be used if the need arose. U.S. nuclear forces, if operated properly, could still play several roles in U.S. policy, depending on how the world evolves:

- Deterring a direct attack on the United States by any other nation that had anything left to lose or perhaps even prevent such an attack in isolated situations

- Defeating an invasion of or massive attack against a critical ally, particularly if U.S. forces are also at risk *and if other means appear inadequate*
- Preventing or punishing a nuclear attack on either U.S. forces deployed abroad or a critical ally *if other means appear inadequate.*

The caveat, "if other means appear inadequate," on the last two points is important because *these situations should not arise if the United States plans and operates its conventional forces properly and chooses its quarrels carefully.* Still, the need to actually use nuclear weapons could arise, and if it does, the United States will have to be able to develop appropriate targeting plans very rapidly. *That is a radical departure from the way the United States has done nuclear targeting in the past.* Implementing such an approach will require *major technical, operational, and institutional changes.*

Also, the last two points have a slightly different flavor than the more traditional expression: "deter attacks on allies." During the Cold War, that expression was a code word for both threatening the Soviets with mutual suicide should they attack western Europe and invoking a more amorphous concept of "extended deterrence" to prevent an unspecified range of miscreant behavior by various bad actors in different places around the world. This notion of extended deterrence was dubious, dangerous, and controversial during the Cold War, and the United States took extraordinary measures to try to make extended deterrence look credible even when it logically should not have. Extending deterrence may be possible in the post–Cold War world, *but it should be done much more selectively and more pointedly in specific situations*—thus, the different language.

Also, of all of the potential weapons of mass destruction—nuclear, biological, and chemical, although chemical weapons do not really fit in the same category as the other two—nuclear weapons still remain the most militarily useful and the most spectacular as terror weapons. Thus, if weapons of mass destruction continue to proliferate in the world and possessing them has any value either as a deterrent or a war-fighting instrument, nuclear weapons are still the best choice, particularly for an "established" nuclear power, such as the United States.

PREPARING FOR ALTERNATIVE NUCLEAR FUTURES

U.S. policy and force structure need to be flexible enough to cope with a wide variety of "nuclear futures." In general, *most of the policies that the United States should adopt and forces it should maintain initially make sense no matter how the future evolves.* The differences lie in how effective U.S. policy is likely to be.

Some distinctly different nuclear futures include

- "nuclear peace"
- substantial nuclear proliferation
- "nuclear nightmares."

The first could occur if the perceived utility of nuclear weapons diminishes to the point where maintaining them appears to be more trouble than it is worth. *The United States should position itself so that it can permit, even encourage, nuclear forces to "wither away" if conditions permit.* Unfortunately, many of the factors that will determine those conditions are beyond U.S. control.

There are serious limitations to what the United States can do to prevent additional nuclear proliferation. Most of the key decisions will be made by nations based on their regional security needs, and the United States has relatively few carrots or sticks to use to influence those decisions. Moreover, regional nuclear balances are likely to be much less stable than the U.S.–Soviet strategic balance was during the Cold War, which means the *risk of regional nuclear conflict could be quite high.*

Fortunately for the United States, some of these regional quarrels are likely to be of relatively little intrinsic interest to the United States, and the United States and other major powers may well stand aside from them. Where the United States does choose to become involved, its military forces, both nuclear and conventional, may be able to dominate any conflict *but not without risk.*

The United States may not be able to either prevent or deter regional powers from using nuclear weapons in local campaigns if the stakes are high enough *for the regional powers.* Even installations in the United States might not be immune from attack. In particular, the

United States needs to avoid relying on potentially vulnerable "critical nodes," such as the "Black Hole" planning center that was pivotal to conducting Operation Desert Storm. *That should be an important concern for the United States regardless of how the nuclear future evolves.*

"Nuclear nightmares" involve potential use of nuclear weapons by different kinds of players—terrorists, "mad majors," criminals, provocateurs, or heads of disintegrating nuclear states—who cannot be deterred or defeated by any of the usual means. How seriously these kinds of possibilities ought to be taken remains to be seen. Fortunately, many of the measures that might help deal with these sorts of situations—better intelligence gathering, use of special operations forces, controls on clandestine nuclear weapons—are reasonable to do no matter what the United States does with its own nuclear forces. Unfortunately, *none of them may be effective enough.*

OPERATING U.S. NUCLEAR FORCES IN THE POST–COLD WAR WORLD

The most important changes the United States needs to make to its nuclear forces are operational. The following are the most important:

- *Rapid response should be deemphasized.* In particular, the United States should eliminate any options to launch ICBMs on attack *if it has not done so already.*
- *The Single Integrated Operational Plan (SIOP) should be history.* The plans discussed publicly for refining the SIOP to make it more flexible do not go nearly far enough and leave some serious institutional problems uncorrected. Instead, a fully adaptive planning process similar to that being adopted by conventional forces should be implemented.

Other operational changes should include a more sophisticated approach to identifying the origin and assessing the intent of attacks, an increased emphasis on "negative control" of nuclear weapons, and an altered view of strategic alerts that emphasizes prudence and crisis stability rather than "signaling resolve."

As long as the United States sees any possibility of actually employing nuclear weapons, the military needs to include them in exercises. There are at least three reasons:

- Training is essential to developing real operational capability and working "bugs" out of the system, particularly for atypical operations, such as using "strategic" nuclear forces to support theater operations.
- Exercises send signals. To the degree that the United States wants to use its nuclear weapons to deter particular actions by others, including nuclear forces in exercises delivers a strong message.
- Exercising with nuclear weapons provides "quasi-experimental" data on how they might be most effectively employed, if at all.

Cutting back on exercising with nuclear weapons could become an important part of an eventual "withering away" of nuclear forces, should that prove practical. However, that should be the result of a conscious policy choice, not a *de facto* one.

STRUCTURING U.S. FORCES

Nuclear Forces

There are several general premises that the United States ought to apply in deciding what sort of nuclear forces to maintain:

- *Numbers do not matter all that much.* A force of a few hundred usable missiles (not individual warheads) is probably adequate for any contingency that is likely to arise in the foreseeable future. A somewhat larger force is probably better for the United States for the immediate future, but largely for reasons other than literal targeting requirements.
- *Practical operational considerations and budgetary constraints rather than "requirements" should be the main determining factors in sizing the force.* The former are real, the latter are not.
- Survivability should remain a paramount consideration in deciding what types of forces to retain. Not only nuclear attacks, but also conventional and unconventional attacks, need to be con-

sidered. Even natural disasters become more of a potential problem as the force shrinks.

- Flexibility is much more important than in the past.
- The force structure should allow relatively easy expansion if conditions demand or further reduction if the climate permits.
- The force structure should be simplified to minimize the number of different organizations with vested institutional interests and the complexity of planning and executing nuclear operations.

With those considerations in mind, the United States should structure its nuclear forces as follows:

- *SLBMs should be the core of the force.* The current plans for submarine and missile procurement combined with START II constraints provide a basis for structuring a force for the immediate and long-term future.
  - Up to 18 Trident submarines or as few as 10 (5 per coast) if conditions permit.
  - 24 missiles per boat, 4 warheads per missile if START II is ratified and remains in force.
  - A reduced Trident D-5 buy with expansion retained as an option, at least for a time.
- Bombers can remain both to provide a backup to the SLBM force and to supplement it if necessary:
  - *The overall size and structure of the bomber force should be determined by conventional, not nuclear, considerations.*
  - START II provides a basis for sizing the nuclear bomber force *if* the United States chooses to retain as many nuclear warheads as START II allows. (Only the number of cruise missile carriers is really an issue.) If not, the nuclear part of the bomber force can be whatever size that nuclear cruise missile stockpiles and bomber maintenance costs and related operational concerns permit.

  - Penetrating nuclear bombers need a short-range nuclear missile to be effective. More nuclear cruise missiles could be needed for large forces.

- *The United States should be out of the ICBM business.* ICBMs no longer offer any important advantages, and they have distinct liabilities that were at the heart of many Cold War strategic debates. Those liabilities could return with a vengeance, *particularly if the Cold War were to return.*

Nuclear command and control still requires some attention, although the problems have changed considerably with the end of the Cold War. Higher data-rate communication systems and more capable planning systems are needed to deal with more complex future situations, but they probably do not have to be able to operate in as hostile an environment as in the past. Similarly, assuring continuity of command is not likely to be as daunting a problem as it was during the Cold War, but there is still a need to maintain a smooth succession if the National Command Authority (NCA) were attacked and to ensure that the new NCA gets the information he or she needs to deal with whatever crisis has occurred.

Conventional Offensive Forces

Conventional weapons now have the potential to replace nuclear weapons in most military roles and should be the focus of future U.S. weapon development *no matter how the "nuclear future" evolves.*

Active Defenses

The current interest in theater ballistic missile defense might actually offer some promise for coping with emerging regional nuclear powers without disrupting the strategic balance among the major nuclear powers. However, theater ballistic defenses must *demonstrate* that they will work and are affordable. Neither is certain by any means.

The focus should be on fielding operational systems with at least some useful military capability as soon as possible. That could both help solve a real immediate problem and alter the dynamics of regional arms races.

Developing theater defenses must also account for other possible means of delivering nuclear weapons—aircraft, cruise missiles, even trucks. Moreover, an overall defense still must be effective and affordable, particularly in view of the opportunity costs of investing heavily in defenses. Fortunately, air defenses are likely to be necessary in any case, so neither the United States nor regional powers need start from scratch. The appropriate balance among all these considerations remains to be determined.

The possible deployment of strategic defenses for the United States is an issue that never entirely leaves the scene. The issues are quite different from those of theater defense. In considering homeland defenses, U.S. priorities ought to be defense against

- aircraft
- unconventional delivery of nuclear weapons
- cruise missiles
- ballistic missiles.

The first two are probably worth doing but *may not prove totally effective, even against small attacks.* The third and fourth may or may not prove worth pursuing, but the United States does not need to decide immediately.

ACKNOWLEDGMENTS

I would like to thank my colleagues Alan Vick, Preston Niblack, Paul Davis, and James Quinlivan for their substantive comments on earlier versions of the manuscript. Dr. Vick's comments were particularly useful and insightful. Laura Zakaras played a crucial role in helping structure the paper and focus the analysis. I would particularly like to thank Patrice Moore for her care and diligence in preparing the manuscript and commenting on every draft. I owe Phyllis Gilmore, Tim Lee, and Ron Miller, in particular, a special debt in editing and producing the document and creating the cover art. Cindy Kumagawa provided assistance and encouragement in shaping and promoting both this monograph and the forthcoming book. Finally, I want to thank Dr. Paul K. Davis for providing funds to cover the production costs of the monograph.

Chapter One

INTRODUCTION

In one of his last major initiatives as Secretary of Defense, Les Aspin called for an overall review of U.S. nuclear strategy.[1] Hopefully, the review of nuclear policy will continue after Aspin leaves office. Such a review is long overdue. Even before the end of the Cold War, some aspects of U.S. nuclear strategy and force posture were in serious need of an overhaul. However, the end of the Cold War—epitomized by the dissolution of the Soviet Union and the Warsaw Pact, the West's erstwhile Cold War archenemies—mandates fundamentally rethinking the role of nuclear weapons in U.S. military and foreign policy. Considering the stakes involved, *there is no more important issue in the security policy arena.*

There is both good news and bad news in the end of the Cold War and the world that fostered it. The most obvious piece of good news is the dramatically reduced risk of a massive nuclear conflagration that would have left the United States, the former Soviet Union, and much of the rest of the northern hemisphere in shambles. Moreover, the end of the Cold War has created a "window of opportunity" in which the changes in the world, the domestic pressures for defense cuts, and the natural evolution of technology in key areas may at last permit a practical working consensus on what sort of nuclear forces the United States ought to retain, how they should be operated, and what military and political utility the United States can reasonably expect from them. In the new environment, many of the most con-

[1]Michael Wines, "Aspin Orders Pentagon Overhaul of Strategy on Nuclear Weapons," *New York Times*, October 30, 1993, p. 8, and Les Aspin, "Nuclear Posture Review," *Memorandum from the Secretary of Defense*, November 5, 1993.

tentious issues of the last several decades are largely moot, overtaken by events. That, in turn, should permit jettisoning much of the ideological and intellectual baggage that has muddled past debates on nuclear issues and replacing it with a more straightforward approach. The practical results should be twofold: a clearer idea of the limited, but important, role that nuclear weapons can play in future U.S. military and foreign policy, and a U.S. nuclear force reduced in size, simplified in structure, and operated more flexibly to enforce that policy.

The bad news is that the world is moving into largely uncharted waters, and the future may prove more bizarre than we can currently imagine.[2] Thousands of nuclear weapons will remain in the world for many years even if the United States and the former Soviet Union proceed with their plans for drastic nuclear arms reduction. The likelihood of some kind of actual use of nuclear weapons may very well have increased. If so, even the most effective U.S. nuclear strategies may prove inadequate to deal with the problems that emerge.[3] Secretary Aspin clearly recognized this problem when he called for the review of U.S. nuclear strategy, citing the fundamentally different nature of potential nuclear threats to the United States in the post–Cold War world.[4] Moreover, the United States may have relatively little influence on the shape of the world that emerges from the ashes of the Cold War, its self-proclaimed status as the "world's sole remaining superpower" notwithstanding. A major conclusion of this analysis is that *the most appropriate strategy for the United States to follow regarding nuclear weapons is basically the same*—at least in

---

[2]For a discussion of some of the possible consequences in the nuclear arena, see James T. Quinlivan and Glenn C. Buchan, *Theory and Practice: Nuclear Deterrents and Nuclear Actors,* presented at the ORSA/TIMS Joint National Meeting, San Francisco, November 3, 1992.

[3]For an extreme version of this view, see Carl H. Builder, *The Future of Nuclear Deterrence,* Santa Monica, Calif.: RAND, P-7702, 1991. For a popularized version, see Alvin Toffler and Heidi Toffler, *War and Anti-War: Survival at the Dawn of the 21st Century,* Boston: Little, Brown, and Company, 1993, pp. 190–203, particularly the quotations from conversations with Carl Builder. Builder raises the perfectly legitimate concern that nuclear weapons will become the weapons of the weak rather than the strong, and that deterrence may not work as it has in the past. That is indeed a possibility, but it is neither the only one nor necessarily the most appropriate focus of future U.S. nuclear policy.

[4]Wines, op. cit.

the short term—*for most of the likely ways in which the post–Cold War world might evolve.* The sobering reality is that there are inherent risks in the post–Cold War world, and whatever the United States does may not prove to be good enough to deal with all of the nuclear problems that might arise. However, there are a number of actions that should at least reduce the chances of catastrophic blunders.

The objective of this paper is to propose a basic prescription for a post–Cold War U.S. nuclear strategy. The principal issues are the following:

- How might the post–Cold War world evolve, and what does that mean for the future of nuclear weapons?
- What sort of military and political value can the United States reasonably expect from its nuclear forces in the future?
- How should the United States operate its nuclear forces to allow them to be employed effectively and appropriately if the need arises, while minimizing the risks of accidents, incidents, or inadvertent use?
- What sort of nuclear force should the United States maintain in the aftermath of the Cold War?
- Are nuclear forces still the most effective instruments for protecting the United States from whatever nuclear threats may evolve in the post–Cold War era? What else needs to be done?

Historically, these factors, which should logically be strongly related (i.e., national goals should determine overall strategy, which should drive military strategy and operational plans, which should provide a basis for structuring forces), have not been. The end of the Cold War may provide a unique opportunity to get these elements of policy back "in sync" in planning for the future.

The paper begins with a brief discussion of overall U.S. foreign policy objectives in the post–Cold War era and how nuclear weapons are likely to fit in. Then, it focuses specifically on the various sorts of "nuclear futures" that might evolve and what they might mean for U.S. policy. Next, it deals with the changes in how the United States ought to operate its nuclear forces in the future and how it ought to employ them if necessary. Finally, the analysis discusses the kind of nuclear forces the United States ought to maintain for the foreseeable future and how its overall nuclear strategy should come together.

THE OVERALL POLICY CONTEXT—U.S. FOREIGN POLICY IN THE POST–COLD WAR ERA

Nuclear strategy cannot exist in a vacuum. It must be the servant of broader U.S. foreign and military policy objectives. Thus, one must begin by briefly considering how the overall thrust of U.S. foreign policy is likely to change in the aftermath of the Cold War, under what conditions the United States is likely to call upon military force as an instrument of power, and what role nuclear weapons are likely to play. The post–Cold War world is already proving to be violent and unpredictable, with ethnic and religious conflicts erupting on several continents and repressed nationalism both fragmenting and uniting countries. Although all nations are still feeling their way, trying to understand how the game will be played in the emerging world, the United States needs to accept three key principles:

- Both its interests and power are likely to be more limited than in the past.
- Both the necessity of and the opportunities for effective use of U.S. military force will be limited.
- U.S. nuclear forces will probably continue to play an important role for at least the immediate future, but it will be much more limited than in the past.

Limited Interests, Limited Power

The defining ingredient of the Cold War was the obsession of U.S. foreign policy with the Soviet Union as a military threat to its national survival, an ideological challenger, a competing great power, and a "confrontation state" on several continents. The perceived competition largely shaped—and significantly distorted—America's views of its interests for several decades. With the dissolution of the Soviet Union and the apparent end of the ideological struggle, along with the unraveling of many of the associated entangling alliances, there are fewer quarrels in which the United States has a compelling stake, especially ones that would justify using military weapons in general and nuclear weapons in particular. To be sure, some of the old dangers remain. Russia and the other nuclear republics of the former Soviet Union still have formidable intercontinental nuclear forces that could devastate the United States if they were so inclined (for that matter, so do China, France, and Great Britain). However, they have no reason to do so. Even if the current political leadership were to be replaced by old, hard-line Stalinists or new militarists, a nuclear confrontation with the United States would probably be much less likely than during the Cold War, except under relatively bizarre conditions that I will discuss shortly.

The Cold War was characterized by various areas of confrontation between the superpowers directly and through surrogates, some of which might have resulted in conflicts that could have escalated to global nuclear exchanges. Europe was the primary example. The net effect was to tie U.S. national interests, perhaps even its national survival, to events in a variety of places that would normally have been of only passing intrinsic interest to the United States.

With the end of the Cold War, most of those entanglements have evaporated, and the United States has much more freedom to select its level of involvement in most of the world. Korea is probably the only area where the vestigial U.S. presence from the Cold War could involve it in a major war, perhaps one fought with nuclear weapons. However, even that has more to do with regional issues, primarily the continuing U.S. interest in persuading Japan to abstain from joining the nuclear club. To be sure, the Pacific rim is becoming an area of increasing importance to the United States and the rest of the world, primarily because of its economic power. However, that should not be a military issue for the United States. Even the emergence of China as a more formidable, economically strong nation that behaves more and more like a classical "great power" need not be viewed as a military threat to the United States or any of its really vital interests, although it is already more of a force to reckon with in the normal day-to-day business of international relations than it has been in the past. In fact, the emerging China is more a creature of the post–Cold War era than a remnant of the Cold War. That makes it a country to deal with, but not necessarily to fight with.

The end of the Cold War has created some new problems for the United States and redefined some old ones. The major new problem, and the one that should have highest priority on the U.S. foreign policy agenda, is helping the former Soviet nuclear republics join the family of nations without destroying themselves or anyone else in the process. That is going to be a major challenge, since there is relatively little that the United States can do to help. Still, it should miss no opportunity to try.

The other area where the United States has an enduring interest that has caused it to go to war in the recent past and could again is Southwest Asia. The dependence of the West and Japan on Persian Gulf oil and the power and wealth that come from controlling that oil guarantee U.S. interest in that part of the world for as far into the future as anyone can see. Throw into the pot Islamic fundamentalism, despotic governments, international terrorism, the Arab-Israeli dispute, ballistic missiles, regimes hostile to the United States, and a high potential for nuclear proliferation, stir well, and the result is a highly volatile mixture with a continuing potential for war.

Other than those areas, the United States has considerable latitude in choosing its level of involvement in the world beyond the extensive economic and diplomatic involvement that are part of being a relatively rich and powerful modern nation. The United States and other nations have been groping about trying to navigate these unfamiliar waters without notable success, as the continuing tragedies in Bosnia, Somalia, and Haiti demonstrate. Questions of how and when to use force, in conjunction with whom, and at what cost are being resolved by trial and error.

The United States has relatively few instruments of power available to it in the post–Cold War world in spite of the hype about its being the "only remaining superpower." Not only has the Cold War come to an end, so also, finally, has the post–World War II period during which the United States held the preponderance of military and economic power in the world. Inevitably, wealth and power have spread to a degree, at least among the industrial powers. Thus, the United States can no longer dominate as it once did. It is drastically reducing the size of its military, although U.S. military capability remains quite substantial. Its economy is not healthy enough to permit much foreign aid. As a result, the United States must pick its spots and use its scarce resources carefully. That means many of the world's problems will be beyond the ability of the United States to deal with. In that context, understanding how and when to use force and what role, if any, nuclear weapons might play is a fundamental issue.

Using U.S. Military Power in the Post–Cold War World

Ironies abound in the post–Cold War world. That era began literally with a bang as the United States, in consort with others, fought a major war in the Persian Gulf and won a decisive military victory. However, the bang turned into more of a whimper as the United States briefly and ineffectively used some of its military forces in Somalia and avoided military involvement in the war in Bosnia and the political crisis in Haiti. These unfortunate experiences involving collective failures by the United Nations, NATO, and various coalitions of nations also considerably undermined the post–Gulf War hopes for enforcing peace in various parts of the world through increased reliance on regional alliances or international bodies, such as the United Nations. During a time of increasing violence in the world, there are fewer appropriate uses for U.S. military forces. At a time when the United States could almost convince itself that it need no longer become involved in major wars, the public flap over "win-win," "win-hold-win," and similar caricatures of U.S. military posture notwithstanding, it finds itself in early 1994 obliged to prepare for the very real possibility of a major war in Korea. Elsewhere, benign-sounding notions such as "peacemaking" and "peacekeeping" turn out to be very difficult and demanding.

Before the United States can develop a coherent nuclear strategy, it needs a better idea of how it might involve military force in general. During the Cold War, the niche for nuclear weapons was clearer. They were the dominant instruments for dealing with the direct nuclear threat posed by the Soviet Union. They were supposed to be the key to giving the Soviet Union and its clients pause if they contemplated large-scale military action in parts of the world that were of interest to the United States. On the other hand, they were tacitly precluded from use in "lesser" conflicts, such as the Vietnam war. The tapestry was by no means complete, and the Vietnam war destroyed any illusion that a consensus existed on military issues and foreign policy. Still, notions about how to use force and where nuclear weapons might fit in were reasonably clear, even when those notions were not shared by advocates of various competing camps.

In the post–Cold War world, even that level of understanding and agreement on the ground rules of policy debates may be absent. However, the United States is rapidly gaining experience both from victory and from the ambiguous outcomes of recent diplomatic and military crises. That experience can provide guidance on the uses of U.S. military force in the post–Cold War world as a prerequisite for thinking about the role of nuclear weapons.

The Persian Gulf War: A "Dinosaur" with Lessons for the Future. The U.S. military victory in the Persian Gulf War and its ambiguous political aftermath may yield some insight into the problems and prospects for successful U.S. military action in the post–Cold War world. The Gulf War had all the ingredients for successful use of U.S. military force: a war that was "right," winnable, and important to critical U.S. interests.

A "Righteous" War. The war was "right" because it had in Saddam Hussein a villain straight out of central casting, a military dictator who slaughtered minorities in his own country, murdered his political enemies, and invaded his neighbors. It also had victims to be saved. While the Kuwaiti royal family left something to be desired as sympathetic victims, identifying with the plight of ordinary Kuwaitis being brutalized by the Iraqi invaders was easy.

A Winnable War. The war was winnable because the Iraqi military was trained and equipped by the Soviets, but lacked their competence. In other words, it was a paltry imitation of the military force that the U.S. military had trained for decades to fight. Moreover, it was incompetently led. Saddam Hussein made error after error in dealing with the United States and its allies and in planning his military strategy. The war was waged in open terrain where all of the advanced U.S. weapons had the best chance of working properly. Finally, through a combination of skillful Western diplomacy and Iraqi blundering, the United States and its allies managed to put together and maintain a virtually worldwide political and military coalition against which Iraq had no chance of winning.

A War in the Interests of the United States. The war was in the interests of the United States because Iraq demonstrated all of the characteristics of a hegemonic power that could have controlled, either directly or indirectly, much of the Persian Gulf oil supply on which the West and Japan depend. Controlling that oil would have vastly increased Iraq's wealth and international influence. Meanwhile, Iraq was actively developing nuclear weapons and other weapons of mass destruction. In time, that could have made Iraq, a nation governed by a regime hostile to the United States, a dominant power in a region critical to most of the world. That situation could have become intolerable and would have been very costly to attempt to reverse.

Short of a direct attack on the United States, it is hard to imagine a situation in which it would have been easier for the American public to support use of the U.S. military, and indeed support for the war was broad. However, that support was also probably quite shallow, although that hypothesis was never really put to the test. Had the Iraqis been less boorish, the war more costly, or the international community less cohesive, the situation could have become another quagmire. Indeed, as it was, public jubilation over the brilliant military victory has been dampened considerably by the ambiguous political aftermath of the war that left Saddam Hussein in power, continuing to test the perseverance of the allies in enforcing their victory. Hopes for a regional security alliance capable of providing a measure of long-term stability in the Persian Gulf area have certainly dimmed, although the United States continues to provide military assistance to some regimes in the area and maintains a minimal continuing military presence itself. The result falls far short of the "new world order" that President Bush had hoped for.

It Will Never Be That Good Again. The point is that *Operation Desert Storm is about as good as war is ever likely to get for the United States,* and it is *unlikely that this combination of conditions could ever be replicated.* Fortunately, there are only a couple of places in the world where the United States has sufficiently vital interests to commit this level of force and sustain the effort politically. Events in Somalia, Bosnia, and Haiti suggest just how difficult it is likely to be to sustain even much lower levels of military involvement and to be successful in more politically complex situations where vital national interests of the United States and other global powers are less clearly involved and political support is less solid.

Future Use of U.S. Military Force? The United States is still groping about trying to understand how and when it can reasonably expect to use military force. Some situations, such as a possible new war in Korea or even the nuclear threat posed by Russian strategic weapons, are reasonably well understood. Others, such as peacekeeping and peacemaking in Somalia, Bosnia, or the former Soviet Union, are not. Indeed, the most vexing military problems so far in the post–Cold War era involve morality and humanitarian concerns rather than the fundamental security considerations that appear higher in the traditional hierarchy of national interests. Deciding how much blood and national treasure to invest in these sorts of enterprises requires a set of value judgments that tends to leave Western democracies ill at ease. On somewhat more familiar ground, another major war in the Persian Gulf, this time with different players and different ground rules, is a possibility as well, and how—or even whether—to fight such a war depends on how the world evolves. Possibilities for use of special operations forces in a variety of situations could arise almost routinely.

There are two general factors, however that make all this uncertainty less discouraging.

- The United States has considerable latitude to "pick and choose" when and how to use its military forces, much more than it did during the Cold War.
- *Relatively few military crises in which the United States might become embroiled are likely to involve even the potential use of nuclear weapons.*

The Nuclear Dimension

Nuclear weapons are traditionally viewed as the ultimate guarantors of a nation's security, or so nations that either possess them or would like to acquire them believe. That is probably still true for the United States, at least against overt military threats from other nations. The United States has a great advantage over most other nations in that the only nations that can seriously threaten its national existence are on the other side of the world. With the end of the Cold War, the major potential threat is gone unless something goes wildly wrong in the nuclear republics of the former Soviet Union. As a result, the relative importance of nuclear weapons in U.S. national security policy has been dramatically reduced. That is all to the good. *A major objective of U.S. policy should be to make nuclear weapons less important rather than more important as instruments of policy.* That should have been the major aim of American nuclear strategy and arms control policy for at least the last several decades.

However, when the stakes are high enough and other alternatives appear inadequate, nuclear weapons still loom as part of the American arsenal. There are probably four kinds of situations in which the United States might use, or at least threaten to use, nuclear weapons:

- To respond to a direct, serious attack on the United States by another country
- To prevent a nuclear attack on the United States, if possible
- To defeat an invasion of or massive attack against a critical ally, particularly if U.S. forces are also at risk, if other means appear inadequate (Note, however, that very few nations in the post–Cold War world rate being considered "critical allies.")
- To prevent or punish a nuclear attack (or attack by other weapons of mass destruction) on either U.S. forces deployed abroad or a critical ally if other means appear inadequate.

This is a slight variation of a fairly standard litany, but in the post–Cold War world, there are some wrinkles. The first point is straightforward enough. It has been the basis of the U.S. nuclear deterrent against a Soviet or Chinese nuclear attack since the beginning of the nuclear age. As a practical matter, it is unlikely that any overtly aggressive act by another country other than a nuclear attack could directly threaten the national survival of the United States.

During the Cold War, some of the most contentious debates on U.S. nuclear policy revolved around how hard the United States ought to try to develop a capability to destroy Soviet nuclear forces in a nuclear strike. The United States was never able to develop such a capability, although it was not for lack of trying, once the Soviets fielded a large, modern, diverse strategic nuclear force. It is possible, however, that in the post–Cold War world, the United States might find itself threatened by an emerging nuclear power with a small, more vulnerable nuclear force. If so, the United States certainly might consider a preemptive nuclear attack if the alternative were nuclear detonations on U.S. soil.

The last two points involve possible U.S. nuclear use in situations other than direct attacks on the United States. There are very few regions in the post–Cold War world that are important enough for this sort of situation to arise. However, if the only way to stop an overwhelming conventional invasion of, say, Saudi oil fields were to use nuclear weapons, the United States might at least consider it, particularly if U.S. forces in the region were at risk. *If the United States plans its conventional forces properly, this problem should never come up.* However, it could have during the early weeks of Operation Desert Shield, and it might again. If it does, it would be reassuring if U.S. policymakers had given some thought in advance to the question of whether the consequences of failure, possibly including large-scale loss of U.S. lives, were worse than the stigma attached to using nuclear weapons.

A striking feature of the post–Cold War era is the breakdown of the stylized, structured, relatively symmetrical notions of escalation that characterized the confrontation between the United States and the Soviet Union. Most future opponents that the United States might face are much less likely to be able to respond in kind, particularly against the U.S. homeland, if the United States employs nuclear weapons against them. That should give the United States more freedom to consider nuclear use under extreme duress, although obviously it would take no such decision lightly, particularly in view of the potential long-term consequences. Still, the *dynamics of escalation are likely to be different in the post–Cold War world.*

The final point specifically refers to deterring, defeating, or punishing nuclear attacks in a theater where the United States is involved. Nuclear weapons *might* be an appropriate choice for the United States if other options are inadequate. However, the United States needs to understand the possible motives of other nations that might choose to use nuclear weapons. Unlike the United States, the core interests of most nations are vulnerable to things short of nuclear attack. A nuclear power might well respond with nuclear weapons to *anything* that threatens its national existence or territorial integrity or does great harm to it. That means the notion of *no first use of nuclear weapons is a fraud* and should be treated as such by planners.

For example, it would be the height of folly to assume that a nation would not respond to a conventional attack with nuclear weapons if the conventional attack were threatening enough. As a practical matter, that means that the United States will have to consider more carefully how to prevent actual nuclear use by other countries and how to make a reasoned rather than a reflexive response should such nuclear use occur.

Accordingly, the United States need not feel obliged to respond with nuclear weapons to a nuclear attack and probably *should* not. A conventional attack, a better defense, or even a sniper's bullet might be more appropriate. *That sort of asymmetry introduces new dimensions into the nuclear calculus.*

Worrying about deterring or preventing nuclear use by adversaries adds new dimensions to planning conventional air campaigns in particular, some of which are reminiscent of the Cold War (albeit with lesser risks for the United States). During the Gulf War, the massive diversion of resources from the rest of the war to hunt for Scuds is an example of the impact that even relatively ineffective terror weapons can have on changing the shape of a military campaign. How much greater might the impact be in the future if nuclear weapons were involved? Similarly, the value of command and control attacks becomes even more problematical. As in the Cold War, they become either a very good or a very bad idea, depending on how one believes the other side will react to a "decapitation" attack and how successful such an attack is likely to be.

Also, attacking (or deliberately not attacking) "value" targets in a nation's economy or the control elements (e.g., intelligence and internal security forces) that keep a particular regime in power could either provide an enemy with an incentive not to escalate to nuclear use or drive it over the edge if it felt it had nothing left to lose. Getting inside the opponent's head becomes even more important and probably more difficult when nuclear weapons are involved. That, in turn, could provide an acid test for some extant theories about the use of air power. In the Gulf War, being wrong was a minor annoyance that really involved little risk. In the future, the consequences of a wrong choice could be much greater.

More fundamentally, its nuclear weapons may not be able to protect the United States from some of the nuclear threats that could emerge in the post–Cold War world. At the very least, the future nuclear world will require much more circumspection than the relatively simple Cold War world.

Sorting all of this out and explaining in a convincing way what the role of U.S. nuclear weapons should be in the evolving world and how the United States can protect itself from the nuclear weapons of others is going to be a major challenge for U.S. policymakers. However, it also offers them the opportunity to replace the "cutesy" acronyms (e.g., MAD, NUTS) and slogans (e.g., countervailing strategy) of the past with clear statements of policy and logic. That opportunity is too good to miss.

Chapter Two

ALTERNATIVE NUCLEAR FUTURES—COPING WITH UNCERTAINTY

The future of nuclear weapons could unfold in a variety of radically different ways, and U.S. policy must be flexible enough to deal with whatever emerges. The uncertainty largely evolves from the competing forces that the end of the Cold War is likely to unleash and the ambiguous signals that it sends to those who either possess or might want to possess nuclear weapons. On the one hand, the United States and the former Soviet Union, having "stepped back from the abyss" and achieved a large measure of political rapprochement, are much less likely than in the past to be drawn into a nuclear war either as a result of a direct confrontation or an escalating regional crisis that triggers entangling Cold War alliances. On the other hand, those Cold War alliances provided the superpowers with both the interest and leverage to exercise a degree of control over their various client states. Absent either the constraints of the Cold War alliances or the protection that they offered under some conditions from regional adversaries, nations that chose not to acquire nuclear weapons before may choose differently now, particularly with the "buyers' market" in nuclear material, expertise, and even weapons themselves created by the economic destitution in the nuclear republics of the former Soviet Union and a more pernicious than usual set of international arms suppliers. Moreover, the traffic in nuclear technology and weapons may finally elevate the old notions of non–nation-state nuclear actors (e.g., terrorist groups, criminal syndicates) from the realm of pulp melodrama to the real world of international politics. Finally, the Cold War "rules of the game" for thinking about nuclear weapons will probably evolve in unexpected ways, which may leave considerable room for creativity in extracting political or military value from nuclear weapons.[1] That sort of "creativity" could lead to great danger if the United States remains poised to deal reflexively with only the sorts of nuclear threats posed by the Cold War.

"NUCLEAR PEACE?"

All could end well. The most hopeful possibility is the gradual "withering away" of nuclear forces as their perceived political utility diminishes, advanced conventional weapons are able to replace them in most significant military roles, and the costs and dangers of maintaining them appear excessive, particularly in the face of competing demands for resources for more useful instruments of power. This is the sort of optimistic future promoted by immediate post–Cold War euphoria, and it might actually come to pass. It is the logical extension of the notion presented in the last chapter that a goal of U.S. policy ought to be to *make nuclear weapons less important rather than more important as instruments of policy.* Eventually, maintaining the infrastructure necessary to support a nuclear-weapons establishment could become more of a burden than it is worth. The infrastructure could decay over time, the result of many small defeats in the bureaucratic wars for budgets and influence and individual decisions about priorities or nitty-gritty things, such as training and maintenance, to the point where nuclear capability becomes a facade at most and could actually disappear with appropriate public flourish if political conditions permitted. The knowledge would still remain, of course, at least in principle, but absent an active nuclear-weapons establishment, the capability would be largely dormant. That may be the closest thing to nuclear disarmament that is possible to achieve, and it might be good enough.

Optimistic though it is, this sort of thing is not unprecedented. The agreements among Bush, Gorbachev, Yeltsin, and Clinton on reducing nuclear arms and maintaining less-provocative strategic nuclear force postures demonstrated very clearly the dominance of politics over technology. With the political will to do so, they overcame, al-

[1] See Quinlivan and Buchan, op cit., for a discussion of some unnerving possibilities.

most literally with strokes of the pen, vexing problems that had defeated more technical approaches to arms control for decades. Moreover, the end of the Cold War illustrated that one of the fundamental tenets of foreign policy analysis, widely believed in some quarters—namely, that change occurs incrementally and that the future tends to be an extrapolation of the past—can be wildly wrong. Bifurcations can occur that make the future radically different from the past. That is why the United States has to be flexible and circumspect about the nuclear future at this stage in world history. *The United States needs to position itself so that it can permit, and even encourage, nuclear forces to "wither away" if suitable conditions develop.* On the other hand, U.S. policymakers must be wary that a de facto "withering away" of U.S. nuclear capability does not occur entirely through "benign neglect" in a world where nuclear capability does turn out to matter.

The problem, of course, is that many of the key decisions that will affect the nuclear future rest with others, and the United States may have little leverage to influence those decisions. Moreover, even if it could, the price might be greater than the United States is willing, or able, to pay.

NUCLEAR PROLIFERATION AND REGIONAL CONFLICTS

The first set of problems has to do with nuclear proliferation and continued nuclear development by the current nuclear powers. The issue of nuclear proliferation is much in vogue now and actually may finally emerge as the sort of world-class problem that many analysts expected from the start of the nuclear age. Moreover, because of the pent up pressures and widespread availability of both nuclear materials and key technologies for developing both weapons and delivery systems, the "nuclear club" could expand very rapidly.

The problem is that regional powers with local enemies are likely to make their decisions based on their own immediate security needs with little concern about the policies of the established nuclear powers. That was going on even during the Cold War, as the Pakistani, Israeli, and South African cases suggest. In fact, Cold War alliances sometimes exacerbated the proliferation problem. In the case of Pakistan, for example, the United States turned a blind eye to Pakistan's development of nuclear weapons since it needed Pakistani assistance in supporting the Afghan rebels in their conflict against the Soviets and the regime that the Soviets installed in Kabul, a conflict that the United States would have cared little about had it not been for the Cold War. Thus, Pakistan, with tacit support from the United States and probably active assistance from China, was able to develop nuclear weapons to protect itself from its stronger regional adversary, India, which in turn was at least weakly aligned with the Soviet Union during the Cold War. Protestations in the Western nuclear strategy literature to the contrary, Pakistan correctly concluded that nuclear weapons *do* have value in war, particularly to a weaker nation "outgunned" by a regional rival.

The India-Pakistan Crisis of 1990: A Preview of the Future?

However, both India and Pakistan may have gotten a sobering lesson about the dangers of nuclear brinkmanship from the Kashmir crisis of 1990. If Seymour Hersh's account of this crisis is accurate, there are lessons both for the United States and for minor nuclear powers.[2] Basically, the crisis developed when India conducted a large-scale military exercise on Pakistan's border in the Kashmir region, where past Indian-Pakistani conflicts had occurred. The Pakistanis responded by moving a smaller armored force to the Indian border to face the Indian forces and putting its small nuclear force on alert. According to Hersh's sources, the United States managed to intervene diplomatically, brokering a military standdown on both sides followed by diplomatic activities that averted a crisis from escalating beyond the control of two weak governments.

There are at least two sets of lessons from this crisis. The first has to do with the ability of outside powers, in this case the United States, to help avert nuclear war in the post–Cold War world. It worked this time because

- Neither side *wanted* the crisis to escalate to a nuclear war and, when given a way out, took it.

---

[2]Seymour M. Hersh, "On the Nuclear Edge," *The New Yorker*, March 29, 1993, pp. 56–73.

- The United States had good enough intelligence to recognize the danger of the crisis and was willing to act to try to defuse it, perhaps because the United States recognized its partial responsibility for Pakistan's nuclear capability, perhaps because it realized that *any* use of nuclear weapons in anger could reduce the inhibitions against future nuclear use for others and make the world a more dangerous place for everyone.
- The Pakistanis had lost their Cold War leverage to resist American pressure, since the United States no longer needed Pakistan's support to prosecute the war in Afghanistan.
- Both sides were willing to accept, albeit grudgingly, the United States as a relatively honest broker to mediate the dispute and help both sides withdraw successfully.
- The relatively modest set of "carrots and sticks" that the United States had to offer—intelligence verification of military withdrawal on both sides, refusal to provide military support to the Pakistanis—proved to be enough in this particular instance.

Absent *any* of these factors, the crisis could have turned out badly, and indeed, a future crisis of this sort might well end in disaster. Others might choose, as the Russians did in this case, to remain on the sidelines, concluding that there was little that they could do, and, besides, the *potential costs of getting involved could exceed the benefits.* Thus, *nobody should have any illusions that the United States, the former Soviet Union, the United Nations, or anyone else will necessarily be able to intervene in regional conflicts to prevent the use of nuclear weapons.*

There are lessons for potential nuclear powers as well. Again, they are both sobering and ambiguous. First, such powers run a great risk of blundering into a nuclear war that they would prefer to avoid, and there might be no one there to bail them out. That might at least give them pause before they choose the nuclear path. However, they may also conclude—probably correctly—that superpower protectors or effective security alliances are going to be hard to come by in the post–Cold War world. If so, these powers might also conclude that acquiring nuclear weapons offers them the best protection against hostile, well-armed neighbors, either because they view nuclear weapons as deterrents as the Western conventional wisdom proclaims or as simply the most effective weapons with which to fight, particularly against rivals that can outman or outspend them on conventional forces. Maintaining even a modest nuclear arsenal with moderately long-range delivery systems might also deter powers out of the immediate vicinity with only peripheral stakes in the conflict from involving themselves directly or supporting intervention by others. Aspiring regional powers might also conclude, along with the oft-quoted Indian defense official who commented that the Gulf War showed that a country could not fight a major war against a superpower without nuclear weapons, that possessing nuclear weapons might be the only way to deter nuclear powers from involving themselves in conflicts in their regions. They may also decide that either maintaining existing nuclear weapons or threatening to acquire them are one of the few ways to get the attention—and perhaps the assistance—of the world community in general and the major nuclear powers in particular. North Korea and Ukraine are currently trying to barter nuclear capability—potential, or at least very limited, in North Korea's case and real, at least in the sense of owning real weapons, in Ukraine's—into political and military capital. During the Cold War, South Africa reportedly had a particularly creative approach in mind to employ its small nuclear arsenal to draw the superpowers into any large-scale conflict that erupted in the region in hopes that superpower involvement would preserve the white South African regime.[3]

New Nuclear Actors: Choices and Risks

New nuclear powers are going to have to deal with at least three sets of difficulties. The first is that the sort of bargaining that North Korea and Ukraine are attempting is extraordinarily dangerous and could backfire with disastrous consequences. That is particularly true of North Korea, which runs a very serious risk of triggering a suicidal war. (Unfortunately, the autocratic gerontocracy that currently rules North Korea may not care, a very serious problem to which I will return shortly.) Countries that could potentially threaten the established nuclear powers directly—Ukraine could be a case in principle,

---

[3]"De Klerk Admits Building of A-Bombs," *Facts on File World News Digest*, Vol. 273, March 25, 1993.

but probably not in practice—play a particularly dangerous game. In these situations, the United States must strike a delicate balance, encouraging potential nuclear nations to forgo nuclear weapons without appearing to reward their efforts to acquire or retain them.

Actually, the Ukrainian and North Korean cases represent opposite ends of the proliferation spectrum. Ukraine inherited a substantial arsenal of strategic nuclear weapons, but not the control mechanisms and infrastructure to operate and maintain them. There is no reason to believe Ukraine has either hostile intent or real nuclear capability, although it does have legitimate security concerns that should be possible to deal with. Also, like the rest of the former Soviet republics, it has serious economic problems, and its nuclear arsenal is one of the few assets that it has with which to barter.

By contrast, North Korea, an aspiring nuclear power, could only mount a modest regional nuclear threat for the foreseeable future, but it is a much more inherently dangerous nation. At the very least, its actions could trigger reactions by its neighbors that could cause ripples worldwide. At worst, it could lead to war. *Rewarding North Korea for being reckless would have very different consequences than bartering with Ukraine would.* Still, either situation could turn out badly.

For example, if Ukraine follows through on the agreement that Presidents Clinton, Yeltsin, and Kravchuk have struck in which Ukraine would essentially give up all of its nuclear weapons in exchange for U.S. economic aid,[4] all concerned can breathe a large sigh of relief and congratulate themselves on a mutually satisfactory resolution to a thorny post–Cold War dilemma. However, if the deal unravels, as it easily could, all sides are likely to be worse off in the long run, and the precedents will be unfortunate. By contrast, the North Korean settlement,[5] if it holds, may do little to prevent North Korea from becoming a nuclear power. Even worse, the perception that the United States gave a lot for a little might persuade other potential nuclear

---

[4]R. W. Apple, Jr., "Ukraine Gives in on Surrendering Its Nuclear Arms," *New York Times*, January 11, 1994, pp. 1, 5.

[5]David E. Sanger, "U.S.-North Korean Atom Accord Expected to Yield Dubious Results," *New York Times*, January 9, 1994, pp. 1, 5.

states that threatening to join the nuclear club is a profitable business. The game proceeds, but nobody is quite sure how to play.

The second set of problems has to do with internal stability and the danger of passing of nuclear weapons into the hands of a hostile successor government or rebel factions within a country. Fear that its nuclear weapons could fall into the hands of a future government dominated by the African National Congress may well have contributed to the current South African government's decision to make South Africa the first nuclear power in history to voluntarily give up its nuclear weapons. India should have similar concerns, as should Pakistan and perhaps even China. The primary case in point is obviously the former Soviet Union, which now has four nuclear republics. At the very least, such concerns should prompt all nuclear powers to pay much more attention to installing safety devices on nuclear weapons and providing adequate command and control systems. As numerous authors have pointed out, that is an area where the established nuclear powers could help, although accepting such assistance could be a bit awkward for the "ambiguous" nuclear powers, such as Israel, India, and Pakistan, that do not publicly admit possessing nuclear weapons.

The third set of problems is perhaps the most fundamental of all. *The kind of nuclear strategies that "worked" for the established nuclear powers during the Cold War may not work for emerging nuclear powers.* Simple things, such as geography and geometry, work against them. The Soviet Union and the United States had the advantage of being half a world away from each other. That translated into a half-hour ICBM flight. The nuclear superpowers spent decades developing warning and attack assessment systems to allow each to respond to attacks by the other's ICBMs and other weapon systems within the few minutes available. Whether either side could actually have responded that quickly has always been problematical, but they at least had some chance to pull it off, thereby presumably greatly reducing the incentive for either side to consider launching a nuclear attack. By contrast, in such regions as Korea, the Middle East, and Southwest Asia, potential antagonists are only a few minutes apart by ballistic missile. That amount of warning is too little to do anything except perhaps alert active defenses. Even the flight times of aircraft or cruise missiles would be short enough to stress air defense systems severely unless they were constantly maintained at the highest states of alert. Mobile missiles alleviate the problems to some degree, but keeping them continuously on the move even in peacetime would be expensive and dangerous. Hiding them might or might not work. The net effect is that *there may be no way for regional nuclear antagonists to develop the same sort of stable nuclear balance that the United States, France, Britain, and the Soviet Union achieved.* At the very least, *effective active defenses would be required,* and the prospects remain uncertain at best. (Interestingly enough, theater ballistic missile defenses appear to be much more "politically correct" to pursue than national ballistic missile defense for the United States has been in the past, so the major impediments may only be technical and financial. President Clinton apparently finds the need for defenses against medium-range missiles so compelling that he is proposing to the Russians that we explore options for modifying the ABM Treaty to permit such defenses.[6]) Regional powers are likely to find a world in which they face nuclear-armed enemies only a few minutes away very dangerous even if they do deploy defenses.

Unfortunately, aspiring nuclear powers may not care. They may see the military arguments for nuclear weapons in their particular situations to be sufficiently compelling to discount what may seem to them largely theoretical (and self-serving) concerns about risk and regional stability advanced primarily by the current nuclear powers. Moreover, some may procure nuclear weapons precisely because they *want* to destroy their neighbors utterly, a nuclear version of the current civil war in the former Yugoslavia. In short, unlike the current nuclear powers, some potential proliferators may acquire nuclear weapons with the idea of actually using them.

The arguments against acquiring nuclear weapons might still prove convincing to many potential members of the nuclear club, but then again they may not, as the emerging conventional wisdom suggests. A lot depends on what happens with Ukraine, North Korea, and other minor or near-nuclear powers that are currently pondering their nuclear futures. For its part, the United States can do all of the standard things to try to control proliferation: tighten export con-

---

[6]Michael R. Garden, "U.S. Seeking to Ease 1972 Treaty Limits on Missile Defenses," *New York Times*, December 3, 1993, p. A7.

trols on critical technology, preferably in consort with other potential supplier nations; support stricter enforcement of the Nonproliferation Treaty; and so on. Unfortunately, none of this is likely to work very well against nations that remain bound and determined to acquire nuclear weapons.

The U.S. Role

The United States also has relatively few credible carrots and sticks available to discourage nuclear proliferation, and those need to be employed very selectively. For example, overwhelming priority in controlling nuclear weapons should go toward helping the former Soviet nuclear republics comply with the Strategic Arms Reduction Treaty (START) agreements, destroying many of their weapons and consolidating the others under Russian control. This is one case in which the United States should offer economic assistance to the republics, including offering financial support to former Soviet nuclear scientists and engineers to dissuade them from plying their trades elsewhere. However, given the state of the U.S. economy for the foreseeable future, there are limits to what it can offer economically, and other states need to realize that. Even worse, given the state of the Soviet economy, such aid would have to be targeted very carefully and still might prove inadequate at the macroeconomic level.

There are also a very limited number of situations in which the United States has a sufficient stake to bear the burden of offering security guarantees to persuade states to give up nuclear weapons. That could be part of a deal between Russia and Ukraine if the parties themselves were interested. The United States cannot really risk supporting Ukraine against a Russia that is bound and determined to bend Ukraine to its will and cannot impose a solution. However, the United States might be able to play honest broker and provide substantive aid to help implement security arrangements that both sides agreed to. Similarly, it could remain an element in the U.S. posture in the Far East if the alternative were a nuclear-armed Japan. Obviously, these are very delicate political situations, and appropriate details would have to be worked out in those few cases in which the option made sense for the United States. Still, the option is there to be used *very selectively.*

Another U.S. option to be used very selectively is either the threat or actual direct use of force. There are a few instances where it might be warranted. One is the direct emergence of another nuclear power that could overtly threaten the United States, as the Soviet Union once did. The United States should make very clear that any such country will be both vulnerable to retaliation, either nuclear or otherwise as appropriate, for any direct attack on the United States. Moreover, its nuclear forces are fair game to be attacked if the need arises. The array of advanced and sophisticated nuclear and conventional weapons that the United States and the other major nuclear powers have acquired over the years should be more than adequate to overwhelm any hostile power that threatens them directly. Operating intercontinental nuclear forces that are secure and invulnerable to attack is a demanding task, one that the original nuclear powers worked long and hard to achieve. It may well be beyond the capabilities of fledgling nuclear powers, and *they may not want to play in that arena anyway.* Of course, clandestine delivery of nuclear weapons à la Tom Clancy and Carl Builder is always a possibility in principle—one allegedly actually employed by the Israelis as a declared threat against the former Soviet Union.[7] Such a threat could conceivably give the United States pause before involving itself in a regional dispute involving another nuclear power, particularly a conflict in which it has no really compelling national interest. However, "suitcase bombs" have their own problems, particularly when employed by a country that is itself vulnerable to nuclear retaliation.

A more serious concern is that a regional power involved in a local conflict might be able to prevent U.S. entry into the theater by using nuclear weapons against ports and airfields that the United States needed to introduce forces or U.S. forces themselves. Threats of nuclear retaliation by the United States might deter direct attacks on U.S. troops but might even encourage a preemptive nuclear attack on ports, airfields, and associated facilities before U.S. troops arrived. Even without nuclear weapons, a major regional power might be able to put U.S. forces at great risk by launching a massive conventional or chemical attack before U.S. forces were fully prepared to defend themselves. Iraq could have mounted such an offensive during the early weeks of Operation Desert Shield and could have

---

[7]Seymour M. Hersh, *The Samson Option*, New York: Random House, 1991, p. 220.

inflicted massive losses on U.S. forces. Fortunately, it chose not to. *If it had, the only feasible U.S. option to protect American lives would have been the use of nuclear weapons against the invading forces.* None of the published accounts of the Gulf War have ever stated whether the United States actually had plans available to deal with such a contingency. Given the practical problems of creating and implementing nuclear employment plans, it is likely that the United States did *not* have them. A repetition of the Gulf War in the future could pose great dangers to all concerned.

In the heat of battle with a lot on the line, a regional nuclear power might not be deterred by threats of U.S. retaliation from launching nuclear attacks against some critical U.S. installations either in the region or conceivably in the United States itself if doing so might have a decisive effect on the outcome of the war (and if failure to do so appeared to make defeat inevitable). That is a problem the United States is always going to have to worry about if it chooses to involve itself in regional conflicts with nuclear-armed adversaries, and a certain amount of risk is unavoidable. Still, there are specific kinds of things that the United States needs to pay attention to in order to minimize the risks. Most important is to avoid concentrating critical assets in a small number of places. A prime example is the so-called "Black Hole" planning center in Saudi Arabia from which the United States and its allies orchestrated the Gulf War. Such a target could prove irresistible to a future enemy regardless of any perceived risks of escalation associated with attacking it. Even critical installations in the United States could be vulnerable to attack, particularly by a "motivated" enemy with a great deal at stake.

Balancing prudent concern about the vulnerability of U.S. forces and infrastructure to attacks on a few "critical nodes" against practical operational concerns and fiscal constraints is a problem that the United States will have to deal with *regardless of how the nuclear future unfolds.* Nuclear weapons just exacerbate the problem. The increasing U.S. reliance on precision-guided weapons, stealthy aircraft and missiles, and other high-technology weapons tends to make it much more dependent on unimpeded information flow, centralized mission and campaign planning, and relatively secure main operating bases for its forces. Deciding how to orchestrate this whole process and protect its critical elements against a determined and resourceful enemy is going to be a key factor in determining how successfully the United States can project power abroad in the "new world."

Ironically, the end of the Cold War could make the United States less vulnerable to being "gamed" by regional adversaries and potential proliferators. As Russia chose to stand aside in the 1990 India-Pakistan confrontation, so might the United States in many future regional nuclear confrontations. Few countries would feel confident that a ploy like that ascribed to South Africa to use a nuclear demonstration to draw the superpowers into a regional conflict would work. Similarly, absent the Byzantine international political linkages of the Cold War, the United States is less likely to turn a blind eye toward overt attempts by nominal allies to circumvent the Nuclear Nonproliferation Treaty and U.S. law to develop a nuclear weapons capability. Thus, not all of the trends associated with the end of the Cold War will necessarily promote nuclear proliferation.

The sort of world that could evolve according to "standard" proliferation scenarios could be quite dangerous, particularly for regional antagonists, but might prove tolerable for the United States and clearly preferable to the Cold War days when U.S. national survival rested on the decisions of others. At least some of the Cold War nuclear threat will no doubt remain, but barring a major political disaster, should amount to little more than "background noise." The violence in the world may well continue to increase, but the chances of one of these conflicts escalating to the sorts of nuclear exchanges that once threatened devastation of the U.S. homeland are likely to be remote.

NUCLEAR NIGHTMARES

The single most distinctive feature of the post–Cold War world may prove to be the serious weakening of the role of U.S. nuclear forces as the primary instruments protecting the United States or its forces abroad from nuclear attack. There has never been any guarantee that the threat of nuclear retaliation would be sufficient to deter anyone possessing nuclear weapons from attacking the United States. It was merely the best alternative among a rather unpalatable lot. However, as long as only a few nations possessed nuclear weapons and those few were controlled by people who were neither suicidal, totally insane, dumb, drunk, or just plain mean, there was at least room for hope that threats of society-destroying retaliation would be persuasive enough that nobody would choose to use them. So far that has worked, and it might continue to in the future.

"Terrorists, Crooks, and Crazies"

There is a relatively new set of potential problems that could be much more difficult to deal with and very dangerous to the United States, as well as others. They are all manifestations of a bizarre future world in which terrorist groups, criminal syndicates, religious sects, or other non–nation-states could lay their hands on nuclear weapons and employ them as instruments of blackmail or general terror; dissidents or rebel elements within nuclear states could wrest control of nuclear weapons from their governments and use them either overtly or covertly to achieve their political goals; or failing governments with nothing left to lose might try using their nuclear weapons either to lash out reflexively at those around them or to extract major concessions from other nations under threat of immolation. These threats are actually quite different, but they do have a major theme in common: nuclear weapons being controlled by people who might not be deterred by the sorts of nuclear retaliatory threats that seem to have worked so far and who might not be as vulnerable to the standard set of military countermeasures as more familiar nuclear actors.

Builder and the Tofflers (not to mention Ian Fleming and other spy fiction writers) have waxed poetic about non–nation-states making mischief with nuclear weapons.[8,9] Such groups would find it immensely easier to buy or steal nuclear weapons than to try to develop their own. Thus, the possible loss of control of tactical nuclear weapons in the former Soviet Union may have substantially exacerbated the problem. These weapons are relatively compact (e.g., nuclear artillery shells, for example), vast in number (i.e., tens of thousands, making accurate internal bookkeeping—much less external monitoring—highly problematical at best), and relatively easy for

---

[8]Builder, op cit., pp. 18–19.

[9]Toffler and Toffler, op cit., pp. 198–203.

knowledgeable people to use because many lack safety devices. They would make ideal terror weapons.

The danger is real, and there is a usual litany of things to do to try to counter it, none of which may be particularly effective. All depend on better intelligence gathering, better technology to detect smuggled nuclear weapons, and special units, such as Nuclear Emergency Search Teams (NEST), Delta Force, and SEAL Team Six, or even standard military forces, either acting to prevent the use of the weapons or to retaliate directly against those responsible if they could be identified. However, Builder and the Tofflers accept non–nation-state nuclear actors as *faits accomplis* They are not so far, and while trying to solve the problem is important, it is probably not as pressing as dealing with the other two kinds of emerging nuclear problems.

Nuclear Powers Coming Unglued

More serious is the danger that either elements within a major nuclear power could gain control of strategic weapons and use them perhaps to start a "catalytic" war or that a failing government of a nuclear state in desperate trouble might, with nothing left to lose, use its nuclear weapons as a last gasp to try to coerce others into helping it solve whatever problems had left it in such dire straits. These problems are potentially more serious to the United States than the terrorist scenario, because both the scale of destruction and the likelihood of the attack's succeeding in the absence of defenses are so much greater. This problem underscores the enormous stake that everybody has in the continued stability and well-being of nuclear powers. It is also, of course, the reason that everyone must be so concerned about events in the former Soviet Union. A real unraveling of that society would be one of the most frightening things imaginable.

The success of Vladimir Zhirinovsky in the recent Russian parliamentary elections illustrates the danger in the starkest possible terms. An electorate that feels that it has nothing left to lose by radically changing its government is certainly capable of enfranchising a loose-lipped nationalistic demagogue who might eventually find his finger on the nuclear trigger. Unfortunately, such a leader, or even a more sober one in the same overall situation, could translate his nation's economic weakness into a very strong bargaining position with the rest of the world. Henry Kissinger was dead wrong when he recently asked rhetorically whether it made sense to allow Moscow to blackmail us now from a position of domestic weakness when it could not when Russia was strong.[10] It is *precisely* Russia's domestic weakness that makes potential nuclear blackmail a very real concern.

Concern about this kind of threat emerging has always been one of the consistent arguments made by proponents of strategic defenses. While there is virtually no chance that even a robust strategic defense would be of much use against a renegade superpower with a Zhirinovsky-like leader at the helm, a strategic defense might be able to cope with more modest threats. The problem has always been decoupling those kinds of defenses from strategic offensive forces. According to the traditional strategic calculus, that decoupling should be even harder if strategic offensive forces are cut as drastically as current plans envision. On the other hand, that calculus was based on Cold War mathematics related to strategic stability and incentives for first strikes. *A major issue in the post–Cold War world is whether the political climate will change sufficiently to break the coupling between strategic defense and offense and allow the major nuclear powers to protect themselves from this kind of threat.*

---

[10]Henry Kissinger, as quoted in Michael Kramer, "The Case for a Bigger NATO," *Time*, January 10, 1994, p. 37.

Chapter Three

THE OPERATIONAL DIMENSION: "STANDING DOWN"

The way U.S. nuclear forces are operated and employed is the area where dramatic change is most critical in adjusting to the post–Cold War world. Some changes have already taken place. More are needed.

The operational problem is multidimensional, but three of the most important elements are (1) assessing attacks and "situations" to support a nuclear response, (2) targeting and employing nuclear forces, and (3) operating forces safely in both peacetime and crises. All three of these areas require major changes from the Cold War days.

IDENTIFYING ATTACKERS AND ASSESSING ATTACKS: THE "HAIR TRIGGER" RESPONSE PROBLEM

The "Old World"

The primary problem that U.S. strategic nuclear forces were supposed to solve during the Cold War was deterring a nuclear attack on the United States by maintaining the ability to retaliate against an adversary who struck first no matter how massive and clever its attack was. That meant, among other things, being able to detect an attack, identify the attacker, alert all of the U.S. forces and supporting mechanisms (e.g., command and control facilities) that an attack was under way, and provide enough information to decisionmakers about the nature of the attack that they could decide how to respond and take appropriate actions. In its most general form, that prescription is largely unchanged. However, the details and emphasis could change quite dramatically in the post–Cold War era. During the Cold War, there was little mystery about who the attackers were likely to be—the list of candidates was very short—and developing sensors adequate to confirm the attacker's identity was relatively straightforward.[1] The real issue was how to provide decisionmakers with enough timely information to make critical decisions and implement them within the few minutes that might be available against a well-designed surprise attack intended to cripple the United States' retaliatory capability. The critical decisions that had to be made before nuclear weapons started going off included whether to launch vulnerable bombers, tankers, command and control aircraft, and silo-based ICBMs; flush various ground-mobile forces and supporting systems (e.g., Rail Garrison Peacekeeper, had the program not been canceled); and take other actions to alert and preserve parts of the command and control system to make sure somebody could control U.S. nuclear forces if U.S. national leadership were targeted in the attack. If a U.S. president lacked confidence in the ability of either U.S. strategic forces or their command and control network to survive a nuclear attack, he might feel obliged to launch a retaliatory attack before enemy weapons arrived.[2] He might make that choice in any case without waiting to absorb the first blow if he felt that he understood the source, extent, and intent of the attack well enough to select an appropriate counterattack option from the menu of choices available to him.

After an initial nuclear attack, if the war were to continue, any surviving leadership would need information about what had happened so far and what options remained, along with means to communicate decisions under very difficult conditions to whatever forces were still available. This last set of problems came to the fore in the late 1970s and early 1980s when concerns about protracted nuclear war were in vogue.

---

[1]Had the Cold War continued and other countries joined the nuclear club, this problem might not have remained simple indefinitely. The proliferation of nuclear cruise missiles could have been a particular problem. (See, for example, Glenn C. Buchan, "The Anti-MAD Mythology," *Bulletin of the Atomic Scientists,* April, 1981, p. 191, inset box: "Origin of an Attack.")

[2]If a president chose to launch ICBMs under attack, a major practical issue is whether that would also oblige him to launch other weapons as well just to make the attack coherent.

Thus, the following were key elements of assessing nuclear attacks to select an appropriate response during the Cold War:

- Timely warning that an attack was under way with a minimum risk of false alarms to support a relatively "hair trigger" set of vulnerable force and supporting systems
- Identification of the attacker, which was relatively easy
- Assessment of the attack well enough and quickly enough to support the decisions that had to be made rapidly, which was more difficult
- Continuing assessment of the situation in the very difficult period after initial nuclear exchanges and perhaps for an extended period during subsequent exchanges.

The difficult factors, then, were *time*, because everything was happening so quickly and a very rapid response could be required; the *scale* of events, because thousands of nuclear weapons could have been involved; and, in some cases, the *environment*, because of widespread nuclear effects.[3] By contrast, identifying the attackers and getting at least enough of an idea about what was going on to decide how to respond were much less difficult, because the possibilities were relatively limited.

The "New World"

The end of the Cold War turned many of these problems on their heads. True, some of the traditional problems remain. A major Russian attack on the United States now would look very much like an attack in the Cold War days, and the systems and procedures that the United States developed to deal with those problems would still have to do their jobs much as before. In other cases, though, the problems

---

[3]Vast amounts of intellectual and material resources were devoted to solving these problems during the Cold War, and a massive literature exists dealing with the problems and potential solutions. See, for example, Bruce Blair, *Strategic Command and Control*, Washington, D.C.: Brookings, 1985, and Ashton B. Carter, et al., eds., *Managing Nuclear Operations*, Washington, D.C.: Brookings, 1987, particularly the following chapters: "Preplanned Operations" by Walter Slocombe, pp. 121–141, and "Warning and Assessment Sensors" by John C. Toomay, pp. 282–321.

could be quite different. First, even in the relatively "standard" scenarios, identifying an attacker could be more difficult simply because there could be more possibilities—more countries with long-range delivery systems, more different kinds of missiles—all of which increases the burden on warning systems to sort out real launches from false alarms, to detect an attack, and correctly identify the attacker. The diversity of possible delivery systems that other nuclear powers might select—cruise missiles, aircraft of various sorts, not to mention clandestine delivery—only complicates the problem further.

However, if one attaches any credibility to some of the more bizarre possibilities, such as a "catalytic" attack launched from an identifiable source (e.g., a specific ICBM silo in Ukraine), but with an unknown finger on the button, relying on the usual warning systems and attack assessment approaches could be worse than useless. As James Quinlivan put it, "The first casualty of any nuclear weapon use should be the presumption that we understand exactly what is going on."[4] What is needed instead is a better "forensic" capability to be certain that the United States can eventually identify the guilty parties with high confidence. Actually developing such a capability, however, could take some doing.

Unlike the Cold War scenarios, time should be less of a problem in the more bizarre post–Cold War scenarios. There is likely to be much less pressure to respond rapidly to an attack. None of the "new" sorts of attacks would seriously threaten the United States' ability to retaliate eventually anyway. If START II proceeds as planned, the bulk of U.S. nuclear forces will be at sea and relatively safe from attack even by a superpower. Depending on the target of the attack, timely warning might still be useful, but *failure to get it is not likely to be catastrophic,* as it might have been had the Cold War turned hot.

The other elements of the equation—scale of nuclear attacks and the need to operate in a difficult (i.e., nuclear) environment—are also likely to change for the better in a post–Cold War environment. Sensor and communication systems are not likely to have to cope with large numbers of nuclear detonations in a brief period of time, nor

---

[4]Quinlivan and Buchan, op cit., p. 14.

are they likely to have to function in the sort of severely disturbed environment that analysts used to associate with massive U.S.-Soviet nuclear exchanges. As a practical matter, that means that the command and control system in general is likely to work much better, although the NCA and various key installations remain vulnerable to attack.

In summary, in the post–Cold War world, the emphasis on warning and attack assessment should change quite markedly. *Timeliness* and *rapid response* should be much less important and *should be deemphasized.* This is an idea that has been around for awhile. Now, its time has come. *Accurate identification of attackers* and *correct assessment of their motives* could be much more difficult and *should receive more emphasis.*

As a consequence of these changes, *the United States should immediately eliminate any options to launch vulnerable ICBMs on warning of attack* if it has not already done so. That is the *single most important strategic policy change* the United States should make in the aftermath of the Cold War. The policy was already controversial in the Cold War and could be a potential disaster in the post–Cold War era. The missiles are very likely to be targeted inappropriately, and even the *possibility* of a mistake far outweighs the risk of losing a modest number of ICBMs. The much-publicized retargeting of U.S. and Russian missiles to points somewhere in the ocean might help marginally against a totally reflexive launch under attack, but if the original targets were retained as alternates, the extra time required to change back to the original targets would probably not affect the ability of the missiles to launch quickly, and it would not allow much opportunity for reflection on the wisdom of the act. Even a *declaratory* policy of launching ICBMs on warning of an impending attack, which might have had a stabilizing effect on the Cold War nuclear balance, would be unduly provocative in the post–Cold War world. Thus, the problem will remain as long as theoretically vulnerable ICBMs remain. A surer solution, and one that will save money, is to eliminate the problem altogether by eliminating ICBMs. As the next section will argue, ICBMs no longer offer unique advantages and have long had compelling liabilities.

TARGETING AND EMPLOYING FORCES: SCRAPPING THE SIOP

Another relic of the Cold War that should go the way of the dinosaurs and airborne nuclear alerts for bombers is the Single Integrated Operational Plan (SIOP) for executing U.S. strategic forces. The SIOP was created in the early 1960s to bring some order to the potential chaos that could have emerged from trying to use the growing and disparate U.S. strategic arsenal that was beginning to evolve in a coordinated way. The objective of creating the SIOP was to employ the total U.S. strategic force as efficiently and effectively as possible, given a variety of possible targeting objectives and practical operational constraints.

The details of the SIOP are, of course, highly classified, but broad outlines of some past SIOPs have emerged in public fora. For the purposes of this discussion, the following features of the SIOP process are important:

- The SIOP is a massive, highly detailed, very rigid plan with very limited flexibility. Past target selection, of course, reflected Cold War priorities and probably still does in spite of post–Cold War modifications to the SIOP announced in the press.[5]
- The SIOP process is long and tedious. Past SIOPs have taken from many months to over a year to prepare.
- There are inherent real and institutional problems in planning a SIOP that make it very difficult to construct a plan that both accurately reflects the range of choices that policymakers might want and is practical for military operators to execute.

In the post–Cold War era, *the SIOP should be discarded and replaced by a more flexible planning process* more closely akin to that used to plan major conventional operations, a process which is itself undergoing major refinement to reflect the need for more conventional flexibility as well in the future.[6] What is needed is not just a refine-

---

[5]Eric Schmitt, "Head of U.S. Nuclear Forces Plans for World of New Foes," *New York Times*, February 25, 1993, pp. A1, A10.

[6]That does *not* imply a "conventionalization" of nuclear operations in the pejorative sense that expressions of that sort have been used in the past. The inhibitions against

ment of the SIOP process. The mind-sets and institutional processes that have produced past SIOPs would probably generate a new set of plans that looked a lot like the old ones. They would probably focus on the wrong targets (possibly even the wrong countries), would not reflect either political leaders' or military commanders' needs, and could be dangerously inappropriate in an escalating crisis generated by some bizarre set of future events.

For example, the retargeting plans proposed by the JSTPS/SAG Deterrence Study Group[7] do not go far enough in some ways, and in at least one area are worse than nothing. The nuclear options are reasonably modest extrapolations of Cold War targeting plans. They may be adequate for a series of stock scenarios but are not adaptive enough to deal with even modest variations of standard contingencies that might emerge in the critical former Soviet republics. There is a fundamental logical flaw in this whole approach to nuclear targeting in a highly uncertain world. A manageable set of preplanned options may well not include what is really appropriate for the crisis at hand. (Of course, there may not *be* any appropriate nuclear option, a fortuitous fact that is likely to prevail in most situations that actually occur.) By contrast, trying to achieve adequate flexibility with "families" of preplanned options may still not be adequate and is likely to overwhelm decisionmakers with more choices than they can mentally digest. What is needed instead is a planning process that is sufficiently adaptive to allow political decisionmakers and military commanders to focus explicitly on what they need to deal with whatever crisis is at hand without having to wade through stacks of preplanned options, dissect what is available, and perhaps try to tailor existing plans to meet the needs of the moment. The only real practical alternative is to decide in advance exactly what very limited set of nuclear attack options make sense, plan those, and make sure policymakers understand their limitations (a daunting

---

nuclear use of any sort would still remain as strong as ever, and the concept of a nuclear-conventional "firebreak" would remain just as valid as in the past. What it does mean is that planning nuclear operations in the post–Cold War era will face many similar problems to those conventional force planners will have to deal with in making forces more flexible and responsive to deal with a more volatile, less predictable future world.

[7] Thomas C. Reed, "The Role of Nuclear Weapons in the New World Order," Joint Strategic Target Planning Staff (JSTPS)/SAG Deterrence Study Group, October 10, 1991, pp. 16–17. This document is also known as the JSTPS/SAG report.

task at best). Ironically, that approach is probably a prescription for guaranteeing the irrelevance of nuclear weapons for anything other than "existential deterrence" in the future world.

The proposed addition of a massive nonnuclear SIOP option combines the worst features of past SIOP planning and outdated conventional targeting. Conventional planning needs to become more adaptive and is moving in that direction with theater planning staffs controlling the process. The last thing that needs to happen is for conventional planning to start looking more like the old SIOP or getting sucked up into that institutional morass. Instead, both nuclear and conventional planning need to move in exactly the opposite direction.

Recent press coverage of U.S. and Russian strategic nuclear force issues has gotten a certain amount of mileage out of the irony that, despite the end of the Cold War, each side's strategic missiles are still pointed at the other. Of course, that is not really all that alarming, since there is virtually no chance of the weapons being used in the current political climate, and if that climate soured, Russia and the United States would probably remain the logical targets for each others' strategic weapons. Still, continuing to target strategic weapons in the old way illustrates the literal and metaphoric paradox of the post–Cold War era: Old ways of doing business die hard, and besides, nobody is quite sure what else to do with the weapons in any case. That is why the process needs to change. Although at first blush it sounds merely symbolic, perhaps even a little quaint, the proposal recently announced by President Clinton for the United States and Russia to agree to target their nuclear weapons at benign ocean areas during normal operations is a positive step.[8] At least, either side would have to take conscious action to retarget weapons to attack the other, which should at least reduce the danger of mishaps.

Replacing the SIOP with a more flexible nuclear targeting approach should be much easier than it would have been in the past. If START proceeds as planned, strategic nuclear forces will be much smaller

---

[8]The agreement to implement this plan was signed by the two presidents at the Moscow summit in January 1994. The idea was made public the month before. (Associated Press, "U.S., Russia Mull Reaiming Nuclear Arms," *Washington Post*, December 7, 1993, p. A19.)

and simpler in structure (see the next chapter on force structure) with many fewer MIRVed missiles than in the past. That should ease the mechanics of the process considerably. Moreover, increases in computer processing capability should make flexible force planning much more practical—so should a decrease in the emphasis on a near-instantaneous response, except for truly "tactical" situations. If any of these should occur, they are likely to involve very few weapons, so the problem should be relatively easy to handle. Also, as in the past, planners are likely to find that there are important practical limits to how much flexibility could be really useful to either policymakers or military commanders. If so, achieving "adequate" flexibility that yields nuclear plans that are appropriate for whatever contingencies arise should be a manageable job.

Some planning problems will be more difficult, however. As in the case of conventional planning, a considerable amount of up-front legwork will be required to have the proper set of potential target bases in hand when a crisis arises that might require the use of nuclear weapons. Thus, while decisionmakers may have more time available than in the Cold War days, when they might have had a very few minutes to select among preplanned options, the planning cycle still needs to be rapid enough to respond to a theater commander's needs in the unfortunate case that nuclear weapons need to be used in an actual dynamic battlefield situation. That sort of problem stresses the entire system of intelligence collection and analysis and campaign planning for either nuclear or conventional weapons. The problems are actually somewhat easier to solve for nuclear weapons than for advanced precision-guided conventional weapons, because nuclear weapons are so much more destructive that they are "forgiving" in the absence of very precise targeting data. On the flip side of the coin, however, that sort of flexible planning is so culturally anathema to U.S. strategic nuclear planning that the current institutional structure may have to be radically altered or scrapped entirely if post–Cold War nuclear planning is going to achieve the flexibility that the new world could require.

OPERATING PRACTICES

One of the first sets of steps that Presidents Bush, Gorbachev, and Yeltsin took as reciprocal confidence-building measures while the

Cold War was winding down was to reduce the fractions of their respective strategic arsenals that they maintained routinely on alert.[9] The United States, in particular, maintained relatively large fractions of its strategic nuclear forces on alert even in normal day-to-day situations.[10] That was a key element of the "hair trigger," immediate-response posture that the United States maintained, even absent a crisis, to deter a surprise attack. Reducing day-to-day alert rates of vulnerable land-based forces as the U.S. did while continuing to keep most of the SSBN fleet at sea out of harm's way is consistent with the general post–Cold War policy that the United States should be following of reducing the emphasis on and need for a rapid nuclear response posture under all conditions.

Safety Features and "Negative Control"

Other steps of a similar sort make sense as well. One possibility is making certain that all nuclear weapons, including strategic missiles, are equipped with safety devices, permissive action links (PALs) or the equivalent, to prevent unauthorized use. The Navy, in particular, has always resisted,[11] presumably because of its greater concern about maintaining "positive control" of strategic weapons—the ability to use weapons when commanded to do so—than about "negative control"—the ability to prevent unauthorized use of weapons—and its confidence that nuclear weapons at sea remained largely safe from theft or unauthorized use. During the Cold War, deciding how to make the balance between negative and positive control was more problematical. In the post–Cold War world, maintaining negative control should definitely get the nod. These kinds of steps are relatively unremarkable and should raise little controversy.

---

[9]Andrew Rosenthal, "U.S. to Give Up Short-Range Nuclear Arms; Bush Seeks Soviet Cuts and Further Talks," *New York Times*, September 28, 1991, pp. 1, 3, 4, 5.

[10]The United States normally maintained about one-third of its bombers and virtually all of its ICBMs on day-to-day alert. It also kept about two-thirds of its SSBNs, about half of which were ready to launch their missiles on a moment's notice, at sea even in peacetime. (Congressional Budget Office, *Modernizing U.S. Strategic Offensive Forces: Costs, Effects, and Alternatives*, November 1987, pp. 70, 72, 86.)

[11]For a contemporary discussion of the merits and prospects for adding safety devices to SLBM warheads, see Peter Douglas Feaver, *Guarding the Guardians*, Ithaca, N.Y.: Cornell University Press, 1992, pp. 232–235.

Alerts and "Strategic Signaling"

Lowering day-to-day alert levels for strategic forces raises another issue, however. Under what conditions should the United States raise the alert levels of its forces, and how would it wish others to interpret such actions? At the heart of this question is the venerable, but somewhat dubious, notion of "signaling." One of the oft-repeated arguments for managing crises is to use strategic alerts to send signals to adversaries, generally taking some action like putting bombers on airborne alert to "show resolve." The United States has done this at least twice in the past, once during the Cuban Missile Crisis when the Strategic Air Command went to Defense Condition (DEFCON) 2, the highest level of alert on which U.S. strategic forces have ever been placed, and later during the 1973 Middle East war when U.S. nuclear forces world wide were put on DEFCON 3 alert. During the Cuban Missile Crisis, the alert order was deliberately put out "in the clear" to make sure the Russians "got the message" that the United States was serious.

There are several problems with doing this sort of thing. First, although all actions inevitably send signals of some sort, there is no telling how the other side will interpret the "signal," and when the stakes are high, ambiguity can be dangerous. Even worse, in the "new world" many potential adversaries may not have the means to receive "signals" unless they can get the word from CNN. Second, alerts themselves contain inherent risks. Third, and particularly relevant to the post–Cold War world, is the flip side of the traditional argument about the value of using alerts to send signals of resolve. That is, that the United States might fear to take prudent steps to increase the alert levels of its forces in a crisis because it feared appearing too provocative. The danger is that failing to alert its forces if a Cold War–vintage crisis recurred could create a dangerous instability, perhaps tempting a committed adversary to strike first from a position of relative advantage. Depending on the kinds of forces various countries maintain in the aftermath of the Cold War, that problem could become more acute if strategic forces are normally maintained at lower day-to-day alert levels.

The solution to this problem is to change the way we view alerts. *The United States should never employ strategic alerts to send signals of resolve.* Rather, it should view alerts as a prudent means to reduce the vulnerability of its forces and command and control network during a crisis, thereby helping stabilize the situation. There is still no guarantee that the other side will interpret U.S. actions that way, but the United States should do everything possible to reinforce by word and deed that alerts, if they occur, are intended to be prudent, not provocative.

Training

Training for nuclear operations is another operational issue for the post–Cold War world. Training and preparation are part of alerts and part of actual war planning. Training is also one of the areas that tends to get cut in times of tight budgets. In the nuclear arena, training is likely to be an issue primarily for bomber crews, since SSBN crews will presumably continue to train routinely. (On the other hand, if SLBMs are to be employed "tactically," training on rapid retargeting is likely to have to be increased.)

Nuclear forces should be routinely included in large-scale military exercises that replicate operations where nuclear use is a possibility. There are at least three reasons why. First is a simple extension of the training logic: If U.S. military planners ever want to consider actually fighting with nuclear weapons, they need to allow planners and operators to practice. That is the only way to develop real operational capability. In particular, using strategic nuclear weapons to replace theater and battlefield nuclear weapons in support of theater operations, has always been an option in principle, but is more likely to be a real possibility in the post–Cold War world. Making that practical will require practice.

Second, military exercises send powerful signals. To the degree that the United States wants to deter potential adversaries with the prospect of using nuclear weapons in particular sorts of conflicts, including them in exercises is one of the best ways to send the message.

Third, exercises offer a "quasi-experimental" way of testing what might work and what probably will not. Exercise experience could cull down the set of possible nuclear missions to a minimal set, particularly as conventional weapons continue to improve. It might ultimately be the key to relegating nuclear weapons to the role of creating political terror and nothing else. Alternatively, if a compelling case for military use does emerge, exercises are key to demonstrating it and fleshing it out.

A gradual decrease in training for nuclear operations could eventually become a major contributing factor to the "withering away" process for nuclear capability. The danger is that, even if the gradual withering away of nuclear capability were a conscious U.S. policy choice, accomplishing it by cutting training could greatly increase the risks of nuclear incidents or accidents if there were a real nuclear crisis. Coming to grips with nuclear training issues is going to be a significant problem for the U.S. military in the post–Cold War world.

Chapter Four

STRUCTURING U.S. FORCES FOR THE POST–COLD WAR WORLD: OPTIONS AND OPPORTUNITIES

Selecting a force structure to implement U.S. nuclear strategy in the post–Cold War era should differ from the past in two fundamental ways. First, the convergence of a variety of factors—the political thaw that was integral to the end of the Cold War, the budget crunch in the United States, and the realignment of U.S. military service priorities—may provide a unique opportunity to structure a U.S. nuclear force that meets the future United States with a minimum of distractions based on parochial interests and ideology that have characterized the decision process in the past. Second, capabilities other than nuclear firepower are likely to become much more important than in the past for protecting the United States from nuclear threats.

STRUCTURING U.S. NUCLEAR FORCES

Adopting a New Perspective

The kinds of decisions facing U.S. decisionmakers are quite different from what they have been in the past. Instead of building up its strategic forces either in size or capability, the United States is now wrestling with the question of how to reduce the force while maintaining "necessary" capabilities, whatever those are perceived to be. Most of the major procurement decisions for the foreseeable future have already been made, although issues remain in some cases about quantities to be purchased. Most major modernization efforts have been completed.

After decades of rancor, most of the contentious issues that have dominated past debates over U.S. nuclear forces are largely moot. For example, while advocates argued the desirability of "hard target kill" capability, technology moved along, and hard target kill is now a fact. The United States ran the race a little slower and deployed less than it could have, but for all the controversy, the end result was essentially a fully capable force. In fact, U.S. nuclear offensive forces are now very mature technically and operationally and can do virtually any of the things that planners have traditionally deemed important for such forces to do. Moreover, the differences among capabilities of various types of weapon systems have narrowed considerably, making it much easier than in the past to substitute one type for another. Except for pathological exceptions (e.g., hard rock caves, some deep underground installations), nuclear weapons can destroy virtually any sort of fixed target, and there never was any question about their effectiveness as weapons of mass destruction whether used against cities or troops in the field. Other features of the equation remain relatively unchanged. "Hiders" still generally defeat "finders," and offenses usually defeat defenses, unless the defenders have a substantial technological edge on the attackers. As a result, there are few things left to decide in the strategic nuclear offensive world except what is worth doing and what should be in the future inventory.

The climate has changed quite radically as well. Obviously, the apparent end of the Soviet empire has removed the primary *raison d'être* for the bulk of the U.S. strategic arsenal. To be sure, most of the former Soviet weapons remain, and if there is any lesson from the events of the last few years, it is that sensible people should be at least somewhat humble in making confident predictions about the future. The December 1993 Russian parliamentary election is a case in point. Still, the new shape of the world should signal a sea change in the way we think about nuclear force structure issues. Unfortunately, this sort of change is hard to deal with, either intellectually or emotionally, for many of the long-time players. Indeed, it is easier to "talk the talk" than "walk the walk." Old "rational" ways of looking at these problems, except for the basic principles established by Bernard Brodie and the early strategists, tend to lead to dead ends. Ironically, some of the factors that were a problem during the Cold War may prove to be part of the solution now.

The defining issue of the nuclear age has always been, "How much is enough?" The U.S. defense community has been elegantly and inadequately grappling with that question for decades. The debate has always been built on a dubious intellectual foundation, as at least some of the participants have recognized. "Objective" criteria or "requirements" have generally been relatively arbitrarily selected goals, typically expressed either in terms of numbers of targets to be destroyed or total damage to be inflicted. At best, these kinds of objectives reflected some collective judgment about what might make sense in quantifying the unquantifiable. At worst, they were cynical ploys to sell or defeat particular programs and win institutional battles. Unfortunately, this approach was generally perceived as the "only game in town," so everyone who wanted to be a player had to be willing to argue about target bases and damage levels achieved after ritual mathematical combat. The game has been played that way from LeMay through McNamara to the last days of the Cold War. Thus, differences between the National Academy of Sciences[1] and the Defense Department[2] on what sort of strategic forces the United States ought to maintain wind up turning largely on whether one believes the target base consists of hundreds or thousands of targets.

The JSTPS/SAG report raises the target set issue, too, pointing out with a touch of condescension that "academics" use different target sets from "serious" defense consultants and the JSTPS. There is actually a grain of truth to this argument, but for reasons other than the ones cited. The real dichotomy has always been between the visions of policymakers (or academics) about what ought to be done with strategic weapons and the nuts-and-bolts perspective of war planners who actually have to translate abstract concepts (or arbitrarily derived surrogates, such as levels of expected damage against particular classes of targets) into concrete operational plans. Now, *that* is a process that broad interaction and peer review of target bases even at a classified level could help solve. Undoubtedly, some past targeting plans could not survive the "giggle factor." Similarly, ana-

---

[1]Committee on National Security and Arms Control, National Academy of Sciences, *The Future of the U.S.–Soviet Nuclear Relationship*, Washington, D.C.: National Academy of Sciences Press, 1991.

[2]JSTPS/SAP, op cit.

lysts who have never been exposed to how targeting really works could find the experience sobering.

However, this is the sort of debate whose time has largely passed. There are serious limits to how wrong reasonable estimates of target bases can be, even those derived from totally open sources. The mystery has long since gone out of this kind of analysis, and the implicit notion that only "those in the know" can do serious nuclear force analysis is simply wrong. Target bases are important on sort of a logarithmic scale: Are there tens, hundreds, thousands, or tens of thousands of nuclear targets? There is very little new insight to be gleaned from protracted arguments about this versus that target base. Similarly, force planning arithmetic, which accounts for operational factors, such as weapon reliability, alert rates, vulnerability to attack, and ability to penetrate enemy defenses, has some value, but in modern times is a relatively sterile exercise. Making these kinds of calculations is a rite of passage that strategic analysts are expected to endure, learn from, and then outgrow.

The problem is that old habits do die hard. Some recent strategic studies that purport to reflect the changed world sound an awfully lot like "cover versions" of old records.[3] Although they make some valid points about the changed world, they make three general types of errors: (1) They argue for larger strategic forces than are likely to be warranted even if the "bad old days" of the Cold War come back, (2) they rationalize a basic force structure (i.e., the strategic triad) that is largely the result of historical accident combined with inter- and intraservice rivalries, and (3) they give undue weight to the sort of mechanistic way that forces were viewed during the Cold War.

The sort of forces recommended by some current studies tend to run in the range of 5000 or so strategic nuclear weapons, roughly half of the current force or even the force that the United States could deploy under START I limits. Even based on relatively harsh assumptions about how the world might evolve, the likely nuclear target sets in most emerging regional powers or even the remnants of the former Soviet Union are likely to number in the hundreds. Even a re-

[3]See, for example, JSTPS/SAG, op cit., and David A. Shlapak and David E. Thaler, *Back to First Principles: U.S. Strategic Forces in the Emerging Environment*, Santa Monica, Calif.: RAND, R-4260-AF, 1993.

grouped set of former Soviet nuclear republics is unlikely to run up a total target set of more than a very few thousand, requiring many fewer weapons than the quasi-official conventional wisdom in the first year or so of the post–Cold War era suggested.

However, even that is "old think." The reality is that *numbers just do not matter all that much.* What *does* matter is the existence of the nuclear force, its overall capability, its flexibility to do whatever needs to be done in a particular situation, and whether the force itself can be operated in a practical, efficient, safe way. Trying to derive a force size based on "requirements" in the strict sense will almost certainly fail. At one end of the spectrum, trivially small nuclear forces, if operated properly, would probably satisfy the basic political ends that nuclear forces could reasonably be expected to achieve. At the other end of the spectrum, as Benjamin Lambeth of RAND once put it referring to the Soviet approach to the how-much-is-enough question, "Too much is not enough" if the whole spectrum of potential military targeting "requirements" in an uncertain world were taken seriously. Even during the Cold War, nuclear forces really had to be (and *were*) sized based on other sorts of criteria. In the aftermath of the Cold War, even the question is not terribly relevant.

The force composition issue has been handled in an even more pedantic way. The value of the triad of ICBMs, SLBMs, and bombers has generally been accepted uncritically. While serious analysis during the Cold War of the relative merits of a triad versus other possible force configurations (e.g., dyads, quadrads, etc.) found it "mildly reassuring" that there was some analytical basis for preferring a triad of strategic forces,[4] such analyses and the more soporific contemporary litanies extolling the virtues of the triad [5] are based on faulty premises about how the various parts of the force actually operate in practice. The end of the Cold War provides an opportunity to do better.

Finally, in spite of reciting the now-ritualized litany about the changes in the world, the need for flexibility, the receding threat of the former Soviet Union, emerging threats of new ill-defined sorts,

---

[4]Jerry den Broeder and Dave Mitchell, "On Hedging and TRIAD Force Levels," *Operations Research,* Vol. 29, No. 5, September–October 1981, pp. 924–930.

[5]JSTPS/SAG report, op cit., pp. 17–19.

and the near-revolutionary improvements in conventional weapons, contemporary nuclear studies give short shrift to the new and focus on the old. Now, there is some wisdom to that: Nuclear weapons could probably solve some of the old problems, but they may not be of as much use in dealing with the likely travails of the new world. However, putting those kinds of issues in perspective is precisely what should be the first priority of a new U.S. national security strategy and its nuclear component.

Politics, Budgets, and Bureaucracy to the Rescue

So what is to be done? This story has an unlikely set of potential heroes. Politics, budgetary constraints, and the scrambling for budget shares and roles and missions among the services—traditionally regarded in the same class as three of the Four Horsemen of the Apocalypse in dealing sensibly with problems of nuclear force structure—may actually play constructive and pivotal roles in getting closure on a reasonable force structure.

First, the end of the Cold War has produced the necessary political conditions for making nuclear weapons less important as instruments of power and altering both international and U.S. domestic perceptions of the amount of attention (and resources) worth devoting to nuclear weapons. The altered political climate manifested itself in the formal agreement to make deep cuts in strategic arms codified by START II and the unilateral "standdown" measures taken by both sides.

That, in turn, has sent strong signals to both military establishments to reorder their priorities and has begun a new sort of inter- and intraservice competition. During the early years of the Cold War, all of the U.S. military services scrambled to get pieces of the nuclear pie, because that was where the action and the prestige were perceived to be. Now, the United States is "building down," and for the first time, the competition seems to have shifted to see which service can divest itself of the most nuclear responsibilities and forces. *If anything, the danger may be that the services,* left to their own devices, *might try to cut too much too fast,* particularly in critical support areas, such as command and control, which have been perennially underfunded compared to the forces themselves.

All of this is a far cry from the Cold War days when the Air Force and Navy, for example, waged bitter internecine battles for dominance and mission responsibilities in the nuclear arena, adjusting their views of strategic doctrine as necessary to advance service interests, and when the Strategic Air Command was the dominant force within the Air Force. Those entrenched and powerful bureaucracies made any fundamental changes in the overall size and composition of U.S. strategic forces exceedingly difficult at best.

However, the fiscal crisis in the United States and the economic collapse in the former Soviet Union have forced their respective military establishments to cut back, reorder their priorities, and in some cases restructure themselves. In the United States, the emphasis has shifted to conventional forces in all of the services. The change has been the most dramatic in the Air Force, which has dissolved the Strategic Air Command, once its premiere command. Forced to make cuts everywhere, all of the services are looking for ways to cut back, and their nuclear components have lost considerable influence in the internal budgetary wars. The net effect is to create a "window of opportunity" when adjustments to the size and structure of U.S. nuclear forces can be made without the usual institutional impediments and, indeed, when institutional processes may help drive decisions in the correct directions.

There still remains the overarching question of what the U.S. strategic forces ought to look like in the future. Absent a compelling set of "requirements" for force size and overall composition, there needs to be some alternative approach. Two kinds of factors help in the immediate future. The first is formal arms control. The second, and perhaps more important, is a whole host of practical operational and budgetary considerations involved with each part of the force.

Arms control agreements provide one alternative approach to choosing the approach size and composition of particular military forces. For example, in START II, the United States and the Russian Federation agreed that, by the year 2003, each side would be limited to a maximum of 3000 to 3500 nuclear warheads deployed on SLBMs, ICBMs, and heavy bombers, of which no more than 1700 to 1750 can be deployed on SLBMs.[6] Heavy ICBMs and MIRVed ICBMs were banned. Thus, this sort of agreement provides general criteria for both size and composition of strategic forces. No one can claim analytical precision for limits such as these. In fact, *this sort of arms control actually represents an alternative to a rigorous requirements-driven process* when the latter does not really converge to a convincing result.

Interestingly, the START II limits on SLBM warheads permit the United States to retain the largest SSBN and SLBM force that it was planning for the future anyway. All the United States has to do is "deMIRV" its SLBMs to some degree, which is operationally desirable anyway in the new world. The United States retains the flexibility to retain enough nuclear cruise missiles to "fill out" the bomber force up to the START II limits or not as it sees fit. *This is a budgetary issue that amounts to a value judgment and a straightforward tradeoff: Is keeping an extra few hundred or a thousand or so nuclear weapons worth the added cost considering the competing demands for funds?* Obviously, there is nothing in START that *compels* either side to build up to the maximum. In fact, *START II is the first nuclear arms control treaty that explicitly acknowledges both in treaty language and the public portion of the negotiating record that both sides need not feel obliged to build up to the limits.* Thus, not only does the treaty provide caps for forces, but also it provides political "wiggle room" for either side to retain smaller forces without appearing to lose face with those who try to "keep score" in these matters. That, in turn, helps foster a climate where budgetary constraints can lead to further reductions in the force unless the counterarguments are particularly compelling.

The political elites, and probably the general populations of the United States and the former Soviet Union, were out in front of the defense establishment on this issue. However, the military services on both sides have found reasons to move in this direction anyway, and the analytical community is still trying to catch up. (Indeed, Russian defense analysts visiting RAND recently observed that Russia benefited from START II because it could not afford to maintain

---

[6] *Treaty Between the United States of America and the Russian Federation on Further Reduction and Limitation of Strategic Offensive Arms,* January 3, 1993, pp. 2–3.

some parts of its ICBM force after the year 2000 and would have had to make cuts anyway. The START II agreement, they said, at least forces the United States to make cuts as well.) As long as the forces in this sort of agreement generally satisfy some sort of "acceptability" criteria, structuring forces this way may be more satisfactory than unending arguments about requirements.

The other major contributing factor in force structure decisions, particularly those involving reducing forces to modest levels, is the whole set of practical considerations associated with operating forces—logistics, support infrastructure, training, and all of the associated nitty-gritty things that make military forces work. For example, there are minimum numbers of bombers of a particular type that it makes sense to support logistically or to operate on a single base. Similarly, minimum practical submarine force size levels can be strongly affected by operational factors, such as patrol length in both time and distance, the size of port facilities, the number of suitable ports, and so on. In the last analysis, these sorts of considerations may be more real than somewhat ephemeral notions of "requirements." Such operational considerations can require considerable detailed analysis to quantify fully. However, data usually do exist, and they are subject to analysis.

What Criteria U.S. Nuclear Forces Ought to Meet

In summary, then, an acceptable nuclear offensive force ought to meet the following sorts of general criteria:

- Be survivable against even superpower-class attacks
- Be effective against a broad enough range of targets
- Be flexible enough to be employed in a wide range of rapidly emerging situations
- Be safe and secure enough to minimize risks of inadvertent or unauthorized use
- Be large enough—probably at least a few hundred missiles, *not* warheads—either to punish an adversary in whatever way is appropriate or to provide crucial leverage in critical military situations

- Be robust enough to overcome unexpected technical problems or emerging vulnerabilities with part of the force.

Moreover, the force should be

- structured for relatively easy expansion if conditions demand or reduction if the climate permits
- simplified to minimize the number of different organizations with vested institutional interests
- sized and postured primarily on practical operational and budgetary grounds.

What the Force Should Look Like

One striking feature of the post–Cold War world is the disappearance of U.S. "tactical"—i.e., theater and battlefield—nuclear weapons. Naval tactical weapons (e.g., nuclear gravity bombs, nuclear cruise missiles) have been removed from ships. Army weapons are being withdrawn from overseas bases, and the Army currently plans for an "all-conventional" future. That means that "strategic" nuclear weapons—SLBMs, bomber weapons, and ICBMs—will be all that remains unless our current course is reversed. As a result, those weapons will have to play roles once assigned to theater nuclear forces should the need arise.

SLBMs. The SLBM force should be the mainstay of the U.S. nuclear force in the future. It has actually played that role for decades, but now its dominance should be made explicit. There is no foreseeable threat to submarines at sea absent an operational compromise that a Walker-like spy ring might produce. Even *that* would have little effect absent a foe with a blue water Navy even more capable than that of the former Soviet Union to exploit the intelligence coup. Similarly, even pursuing the elusive "technological breakthrough" that might make submarines vulnerable requires both a major research establishment and a significant military capability to exploit. This seems even less likely in the "new world" than it did in the old. In port, of course, the boats remain potentially vulnerable to direct attack by nuclear or conventional weapons or, perhaps, to commandos or terrorists. That is why maintaining most of the SSBN fleet at sea remains a sensible policy as long as the United States retains a nuclear force. Probably the main danger to the SSBN force would be reducing it to the point where the impact of accidents at sea becomes significant. On the other hand, the British and French have managed to operate successfully for years with much smaller SSBN forces than the United States has been willing to consider so far, so the problem might not be all that great.

The missiles themselves are capable of doing virtually anything that nuclear weapons need to do. The combination of range and accuracy that the large Trident D-5 missile provides remove any limitations that past SLBMs might have had in lethality against the full spectrum of target types or achieving full coverage of potential targets from likely SSBN patrol zones. Communications with SSBNs have improved considerably over the history of the force and should not be a limiting factor in the future, particularly absent the stressing environment of a large-scale global nuclear exchange. Thus, the U.S. SLBM force should be capable of doing virtually anything that nuclear forces can do in the future.

Currently, 18 Trident submarines are either in the force or under construction. Each is designed to carry 24 missiles. If each were equipped with four warheads, half the current loading, that would produce a force of 1728 SLBM warheads, which conforms to the START II limits. The general objective within those limits should be to keep as many *missiles* (as opposed to warheads) available as possible. That provides the greatest flexibility to spread SLBM warheads out in space and time if that were to prove necessary in some future crisis. It comes at extra cost compared to reducing the number of submarines or the number of missiles per submarine, but the extra cost is worth it until the new shape of the world becomes clearer.

Depending on how events unfold, the SLBM force could be allowed to "wither away" by not backfitting the older Trident submarines with D-5 missiles or even letting the number of submarines decrease as the older boats need to be either refurbished or retired.[7] A minimum practical number of SSBNs is probably about ten, five operat-

[7]For a discussion of some of the options, see Congress of the United States, Congressional Budget Office, *Rethinking the Trident Force*, July 1993, and "Trident Production to be Halved," *Navy News & Undersea Technology*, Vol. 10, No. 19, May 17, 1993.

ing out of each of two home ports. Eventually, even that could be relaxed if the political climate allowed.

Conversely, if the United States has to expand its nuclear forces, simply reMIRVing the missiles and maintaining, or even enlarging, the submarine force over time remains an option. Thus, the SLBM force should play the dominant role in any future U.S. nuclear offensive force.

Heavy Bombers. If the United States chooses to retain other nuclear forces, whether to maintain a larger force, hedge against some systemic failure in the SLBM force, or provide some slightly different capabilities, that force should consist of bomber weapons. The United States needs to retain a substantial bomber force for conventional operations regardless of what happens in the nuclear arena. In fact, RAND analysis showed that even before the Cold War ended, conventional needs should be the dominant factor in determining the size and composition of the U.S. heavy bomber force. Since all of the current U.S. bombers were designed primarily for nuclear operations, retaining some of them for either dual use as nuclear or conventional bombers or as dedicated nuclear delivery platforms should pose few problems.

Since President Bush made the decision to limit the B-2 buy to 20 aircraft, each of which could carry a combination of 16 nuclear bombs or short-range missiles, dual-capable B-2s could add just over 300 nuclear weapons to the U.S. force. The United States could expand the force as much as it chooses to up to the overall START II limits by adding nuclear cruise missiles to the force. Depending on how large a nuclear cruise-missile force the United States chooses to deploy and what weapon loadings it finally settles on for the bombers, it could retain a force of about 50 to 100 heavy bombers as nuclear cruise-missile carriers. Moreover, as the Gulf War demonstrated, nuclear cruise-missile carriers can be used to deliver conventional cruise missiles as well.

Retaining a nuclear bomber force has some advantages in any case. To the extent that one attaches weight to the arguments about the value of maintaining a hedge against the possibility of something going wrong with other parts of the strategic force, bombers complement ballistic missiles, because bombers and their weapons depend for the most part on different physical phenomena and critical technologies than ballistic missiles. Thus, a common technical failure would be unlikely. Similarly, each requires different counters, whether active defenses or counteroffensive attacks, so a combined force would be much harder for an enemy to defeat. Also, bombers may have some advantages for some kinds of military missions, such as engaging mobile forces. Since bombers are going to have to be able to do that anyway with conventional weapons, retaining the ability to use nuclear weapons if conventional firepower proves inadequate is a logical use of bombers.

Although most of the things that a nuclear bomber force needs either exist now or will soon, some improvements may be needed:

- *A short-range nuclear missile.* Since current SRAM-As have safety problems and since President Bush canceled its successor, SRAM II, penetrating bombers will have no short-range nuclear standoff weapons. Without them, attacking defended targets could be risky.
- *More nuclear cruise missiles.* President Bush capped the Advanced Cruise Missile (ACM) buy at a few hundred. The United States will either have to retain its current nuclear air-launched cruise missiles (ALCM-Bs) or keep the ACM line open if it wants to deploy the largest nuclear bomber force allowed by START II.

Although bombers could conceivably continue to plan to fly over targets and drop nuclear gravity bombs, a prudent planner should probably assume that any target important enough to attack would also be important enough for an enemy to defend. Moreover, an opponent serious enough to warrant a U.S. nuclear attack would probably be capable of acquiring some modern terminal defenses. Situations could exist where it would be easier to suppress the defenses with some kind of missile and then attack the target with nuclear gravity bombs than simply to attack the target with a nuclear missile in the first place, but such cases should be the exception in the post–Cold War world. Without a SRAM-like nuclear missile, penetrating nuclear bombers will have to be used much more carefully. That might be acceptable in the current climate, but the choice should be made consciously, not by default. There are also some practical concerns about maintaining the bombers' nuclear certification as they are modified for conventional operations. Relaxing the old rules on nuclear hardness may well be appropriate, since the environment in which the bombers would have to operate is likely to be less severe than that contemplated for executing the SIOP during the Cold War.

The cruise missile issue is different. The real question is how much the United States values retaining a sizable (more than about 1000 nuclear weapons) bomber force as START II permits. There is no particularly compelling strategic reason unless the United States wants to retain a serious, as opposed to a rhetorical, hedge against the failure of the SSBN force or still contemplates waging a Cold War–style nuclear campaign against a Soviet-class adversary. As the last chapter suggested, this choice is a straight value judgment.

ICBMs. *The United States should be out of the ICBM business.* ICBMs add no unique capabilities to the strategic force and do have unique disadvantages. Eliminating them would save some money; avoid the need to replace the current MIRVed ICBMs with START II-compliant, single-warhead missiles; allow dismantling some supporting infrastructure; and eliminate some of the entrenched institutional interests that have muddled strategic debates over the years. More important, if the Cold War were to resume, vulnerable silo-based ICBMs would again become a distinct liability, because they invite a preemptive strike in a crisis *even if both sides retained substantial reserve forces after such a strike.* The danger is not, and never was, that postulated in the so-called "Nitze scenario," that the United States would be forced to "surrender" after such an exchange because the correlation of forces had shifted to the other side. That contention was absurd then and is even more so now. Rather, the danger is just the opposite: that U.S. decisionmakers would "freak out" and launch a massive retaliatory strike even if the strategic logic of the situation did not require it, thus leading to uncontrolled escalation. Now, some authors would call the danger of such a scenario a reason to keep ICBMs, because the very provocative nature of the attack would act as a deterrent. Warner and Ochmanek picked up that familiar theme, saying that it may "seem perverse to regard this [i.e., the fact that attacking U.S. ICBMs would require a massive attack on U.S.

soil] as an advantage."[8] They are partly right: It not only *seems* perverse, it *is* perverse. That is deterrence at too high a price, and judging from the way U.S. targeteers have viewed this kind of thing in the past, the logic probably would not work if put to the test in a stressed environment. Why run the experiment?

ICBMs were at the heart of most of the contentious battles of the Cold War: silo vulnerability, hard target kill, launch-on-warning in all of its different flavors, countless bizarre ICBM basing schemes, and some aspects of strategic defense. During much of this time, they were more of a liability than an asset, particularly as other parts of the strategic force improved to offset the original technical advantages that ICBMs initially offered (e.g., accuracy, ease of communication, relatively low cost). During that time, ICBMs had enough institutional support to remain part of the landscape. Now, things are quite different. With the dissolution of the Strategic Air Command, ICBMs have no natural home. At the moment, Air Force Space Command has inherited them, but that is not a particularly compelling match. In short, ICBMs rank very low on the Air Force's priority list for the post–Cold War world, as they should. Now is the time to get rid of them.

Even under the worst imaginable circumstances (and they *are* really hard to imagine), in which SSBNs eventually became vulnerable and bombers and cruise missiles were rendered ineffective, there would *still* be no convincing argument for maintaining the ICBM establishment as it now exists. If that were to occur and the United States still felt the need to maintain a secure, effective strategic nuclear force, it would have to come up with a system quite different from anything entertained in the past. In that case, having an ongoing ICBM establishment would be more of a hindrance than a help, because it would have a vested interest in business as usual. Moreover, *maintaining an infrastructure unique to ICBMs would be unduly expensive* and unwarranted in the absence of an immediate need. The industrial infrastructure to build missiles and their key components—rocket engines, guidance systems, critical materials—will continue to exist no matter what happens to ICBMs, because other

---

[8]Edward L. Warner III and David A. Ochmanek, *Next Moves: An Arms Control Agenda for the 1990s*, Council on Foreign Relations Press, New York, 1989, p. 51.

kinds of systems require similar technologies. Thus, any sort of argument that says the United States needs to maintain an ICBM force and all of its related infrastructure as a hedge against some future failure of the rest of the force is specious. It gives the whole notion of "hedging" a bad name.

There would be a certain irony to eliminating ICBMs now. Unless the Cold War resumes, their survivability is not in much doubt. Moreover, if there is any need for precise use of nuclear warheads one at a time delivered quickly from secure U.S. bases, ICBMs could do that. However, SLBMs could do essentially the same thing, except that they would have to send at least four warheads at a time. In situations where this might come up, the difference hardly matters. At worst, it would mean wasting a couple of warheads, since it would cost a single booster in any case. Bombers could deliver one weapon at a time and could do it quickly if they were already operating in the target area. Moreover, SLBMs and bombers offer more advantages for the long term, whatever that might bring, and should remain part of the force in any case. Maintaining a meaningful "dyad" of SLBMs and bombers is a better investment than trying to preserve a three-legged skeleton force and infrastructure. The relatively modest cost savings that would result from eliminating ICBMs are still that: savings. Moreover, eliminating ICBMs would eliminate the need to argue over *conventional* ICBMs, an overly expensive solution to any problem one can imagine, but one that has emerged inevitably yet again in the new climate. Thus, even though the hour is late, ICBMs should now become history.

Command and Control. At least two areas of support deserve comment: command and control and nuclear weapons. Command and control systems for nuclear weapons will deserve some additional attention in the future. During the Cold War, the major command and control problems were associated primarily with responding to a large-scale nuclear attack that might destroy U.S. forces before they could be used, kill those who could authorize use of nuclear weapons, or destroy or impede critical communication systems needed to disseminate orders to attack. The initial emphasis was on making a decision quickly from among a limited set of choices and transmitting a terse implementation message rapidly to all of the forces before the weight of the attack overwhelmed communications systems and other critical links in the chain. Later, there was more interest in fighting a protracted nuclear war in which the command and control system, as well as the strategic forces themselves, would have to survive and continue to function—and perform more complicated tasks—in a very hostile environment for as long as necessary to terminate the conflict.[9]

While the end of the Cold War has not entirely eliminated those problems, it has reduced their relative importance. However, flexible use of nuclear weapons in the future, if that proves necessary, will require much more adaptive planning capability and, to handle bizarre cases that might arise, a "forensic" capability that would permit a much more fine-grained assessment of who the attackers might be than current warning and nuclear detection sensors can provide. I discussed these problems earlier. In addition, higher-data-rate, worldwide communications are likely to be needed to send more detailed targeting information to forces. This is a very different problem from sending a short launch message through a very disturbed environment, which has been the primary focus of strategic communication systems for many years. The good news is that *U.S. conventional forces will need these same capabilities*, so providing them for strategic forces should not unduly burden the overall U.S. defense posture. Moreover, it is much less likely that the United States would have to cope with either a massive attack on facilities in its homeland or an environment disrupted by nuclear blasts or large-scale communications jamming for an extended period of time.

Assuring the survival of command, control, and communications systems remains a matter of some concern as well. While not the cutting edge issue that it was during the Cold War, survival and continuity of command should not be taken totally for granted in the post–Cold War world. In fact, reducing the alert levels of airborne command posts during the Bush administration was arguably a much more significant step—and a riskier one—than removing the bomber force from day-to-day alert. Damaging the U.S. nuclear command and control system could ultimately affect a larger part of the U.S. strategic force than a successful attack on bomber bases.

---

[9]Providing adequate command and control capability during a protracted nuclear war also generated a massive literature. See, for example, Blair, op cit., pp. 272–280, and Alan J. Vick, "Post-Attack Strategic Command and Control Survival: Options for the Future," *Orbis*, Spring, 1985, pp. 95–117, particularly pp. 107–117.

The United States need not be paranoid about the dangers, but some prudent steps for preserving nuclear command and control in the post–Cold War era might include the following:

- Steps to preserve sensor data in the event of an attack on the NCA, major headquarters, or planning centers so that surviving authorities can figure out what happened and decide how to respond
- Maintenance of procedures for rapid, efficient presidential succession in the event of an attack on the president
- An ability to reconstitute planning centers if major facilities are destroyed.

Providing at least this level of command continuity should be relatively straightforward compared to the Cold War days but still demands at least a modicum of attention. The same applies to other sorts of facilities where major capabilities are centralized and a "single point failure" could have a dramatic impact on U.S. operational capabilities. The B-2 base at Whiteman AFB, campaign planning centers such as the "Black Hole" in Saudi Arabia used during the Gulf War, and similar planning centers in the United States are examples.

On the other hand, the post–Cold War command and control environment poses some problems that are different from either the standard problem of reacting quickly to a massive nuclear attack or operating for an extended period in a protracted nuclear war. Theater commanders may face some of the same problems—potential vulnerability to nuclear, chemical, biological, conventional, or unconventional attack. That probably means that theater commands should continue to maintain airborne command posts as backups to ground-based installations. It also probably means relying heavily on processing and analyzing data in the United States away from the fray, so that command centers in the theater can be somewhat more austere and perhaps be made less vulnerable. That, in turn, is likely to require a *massive increase in global communications capacity* far beyond the needs of whatever U.S. nuclear forces remain.

Relying on installations in the United States to be an integral part of planning and executing major theater campaigns makes it even less likely that U.S. soil will remain a sanctuary even in the absence of a large-scale nuclear war. However, the kind of threat they are likely to face is different. While overt conventional or nuclear attacks remain a possibility, use of special operations forces is more likely and more of a threat *if U.S. command facilities are either concentrated in a very small number of relatively unprotected installations or a few improperly operated ground-mobile alternates.* Getting in and out of the United States is trivial for small groups of professionals. So is getting around and getting close to even very secure facilities. If those facilities can be attacked successfully with relatively light weapons, the temptation could be too great. The key to success is developing effective operational concepts for the command and control system. In general, the United States cannot "outproliferate" threats, although it can certainly come closer in the post–Cold War world than it could before.

There are three critical elements that apply both to the problem of military operations in general and possible nuclear operations in particular in the post–Cold War era:

- Preserve and proliferate *data*
- Protect bases from nonnuclear attack
- Move decisionmakers to the data inside the United States or be able to save the data and send it to them when it is convenient.

Having terminals from various satellites and other sources, in addition to databases of different sorts, at a number of protected military facilities and a few covert locations is a Cold War notion that might be more useful in the post–Cold War world. There is nothing particularly magic about any specific number of alternative sites, nor is there any analysis that would lead to a credible number. Rather, the general idea is to make a coordinated tactical assault difficult in a situation involving less than a major nuclear war and maintaining the capability to orchestrate an eventual, deliberate response even in the event of a major nuclear attack. As in other areas, the determining factors in working out the details should be operational practicality and cost. There are limits to what can be done with certainty, so in the last analysis, applying a common-sense test is probably the most reasonable way to proceed.

All of this has several implications for changes to the strategic command and control system:

- Airborne command posts, *other than the National Emergency Airborne Command Post* (NEACP), are less necessary than during the Cold War.
- Technology improvements should make proliferating ground terminals and databases cheaper and easier.
- The reduced need for rapid communications in a nuclear environment both greatly eases communication problems and reduces the need for airborne relay aircraft.

That means Looking Glass and the airborne relay and launch control aircraft are probably no longer necessary, particularly if ICBMs are eliminated. TACAMO aircraft are less necessary as well, considering the redundant systems already available that should work well in a clear environment. Even in a disturbed environment, the Milstar I satellite that has already been launched and the second Milstar I that is scheduled for launch next year should provide considerable capability to deal with "worst case" nuclear scenarios. Maintaining TACAMO aircraft at lower alert levels is another option as a backup. In any case, the *problems are easier and the solutions are both different and cheaper in the post–Cold War era.*

Finally, organizational changes seem in order as well. *There is probably no need for a Strategic Command.* Its functions and systems can be effectively absorbed into the other theater commands. That will ease the command and control problems for *both* nuclear and conventional operations in the future.

Thus, some operational and technical changes in command and control are warranted for coping with the post–Cold War world. These are the kinds of things that can "slip through the cracks" unless someone pays attention to them, and that could cause real problems.

Nuclear Weapons Development. By contrast, the United States probably does *not* need to develop any new nuclear warhead designs. It is not that there is no room to develop new weapons. In spite of the relative maturity of the science and art of nuclear warhead design in the United States, possibilities continue to exist for "tailoring" nuclear warheads for specific offensive, and even defensive, applications. Rather, the value of doing so has diminished substantially, particularly in view of the dramatic improvements in the effectiveness of conventional weapons for applications where a stiletto is more appropriate than a sledgehammer. The U.S. sledgehammers are already in place. The stilettos are getting sharper all the time. Thus, the cost of maintaining a nuclear weapon design and testing establishment of anything like the size and vigor of times past is not warranted in the post–Cold War world. A residual capability for understanding and maintaining nuclear weapons is necessary. What is *not* necessary is maintaining a weapon design capability. Designing new nuclear weapons means continuing to conduct nuclear tests. This is the time to try a nuclear test ban. The absolute worst that can happen is that, some years from now, the United States might have to reconstitute its nuclear weapon design capability. In an austere environment, the risks are worth taking.

OTHER CAPABILITIES FOR DEALING WITH NUCLEAR THREATS

As noted earlier, one of the major ways that the post–Cold War world differs from the "nuclear past" is the relative decline in importance of U.S. nuclear offensive forces as the appropriate response to potential nuclear threats. Of course, that was the goal of strategic defense advocates during the Cold War. The difference is that strategic offense and defense have always been intimately coupled, which was at the heart of all the strategic defense debates. By contrast, *many of the steps that might help deal with some of the emerging nuclear threats are largely independent of whatever nuclear forces the United States chooses to maintain.* These include (1) improved intelligence and "nuclear sleuthing," (2) improved conventional weapons, and (3) active defenses, particularly theater defenses.

Intelligence and Nuclear Sleuthing

A case in point is the whole set of devices, policies, and procedures that might be of use for keeping terrorist bombs out of the country, preempting such efforts if possible, and punishing them if it is not. *These kinds of things are unambiguously desirable no matter what else the United States does in the nuclear arena.* Similarly, the ability to assign responsibility for actual nuclear use to avoid catalytic war or other mischief making can only help. However, *the United States needs to be prepared to accept the possibility that none of these actions will be effective enough to offer real protection from novel nuclear threats.* Moreover, like all other programs in the post–Cold War era, they will have to compete for scarce resources, so even good ideas are going to be subjected to considerable scrutiny. This is an area that still remains relatively conceptual and fertile for exploration, so there is considerable room for new ideas to be examined.

Some possibilities, such as using the nuclear weapon laboratories' expertise to trace the origins of a bomb by analyzing residue from its nuclear materials and making inferential judgments about its design, might actually work. Even that kind of nuclear sleuthing, however, could become considerably more complicated as bomb designs and even nuclear material are shared and passed around. For example, a Pakistani bomb design, allegedly of Chinese origin, is supposed to be making the rounds in the Middle East. The chain of blame could be a long one if such a bomb were ever actually used.

Particularly dubious are any schemes for coping with nuclear threats that depend critically on dramatic improvements in U.S. intelligence capability. There are limits to what can be reasonably expected, particularly in recruiting human sources in very hostile countries, such as North Korea, Iraq, and Iran. Technical collection systems are good at some things, less good at others. Moreover, one must assume that fiscal austerity will affect the intelligence community as well, which is likely to mean less rather than more technical collection in the future and more competition for the collection resources that do exist. In a similar vein, at a time when the need for intelligence analysis is probably increasing, the Clinton administration is committed to significantly reducing the number of analysts in the U.S. intelligence community. Granted, there is almost always room to trim and tighten up any bureaucracy. Still, given the breath-conserving performance of the intelligence community in correctly assessing Iraq's potential nuclear capacity and even in fully understanding the nuclear weapon program in the former Soviet Union after decades of effort, it is difficult to be sanguine about its ability to deal with the much more difficult problems of future nuclear proliferation. The problems are simply extraordinarily difficult, and policymakers should have no illusions about their chances of success.

Conventional Weapons

Intelligence problems are likely to be particularly important limiting factors in mounting direct attacks against nuclear facilities and forces. For example, the sorts of advanced conventional weapons that the United States and other countries already have and are continuing to develop to attack the full spectrum of targets could be used effectively against many kinds of nuclear targets if they could be located and characterized in sufficient detail. However, finding mobile nuclear weapons is likely to be very difficult, as the Scud-hunting experiences in the Gulf War showed. Even identifying fixed nuclear installations and characterizing them well enough to attack effectively with precision-guided munitions can be very demanding, a lesson the U.S. defense community is only now beginning to appreciate fully. The good news is that *the U.S. military needs to develop most of these capabilities for regular military operations even against foes that do not have nuclear arms.* The bad news is that capabilities that are adequate to deal with conventional conflicts *may not be good enough against a nuclear-armed foe.*

Even if the basic technical and operational problems can be solved, relying on conventional weapons to defeat nuclear weapons does have some fundamental limitations that some of the more zealous advocates of precision-guided conventional weapons either misunderstand or choose to ignore. First is the notion of risk. If the United States is attacking another country's nuclear weapons, a failed attack is likely to result in the surviving weapons being used against the United States, its troops, or its allies. Thus, the consequences of failure could be considerable, which means that deliberately choosing to use a conventional weapon rather than a potentially more effective nuclear weapon—"blunt instrument" though it is—could be a tough call in spite of possible concerns about changing the "rules of the game." Moreover, the other side is certainly going to consider a potentially lethal conventional attack on its nuclear forces every bit as provocative as a nuclear attack and is likely to react accordingly. An emerging nuclear power with a relatively small nuclear stockpile is likely to be particularly sensitive to such concerns.

What that means as a practical matter is that such assertions as the one in the JSTPS/SAG report[10] that conventional attacks on nuclear weapons are a means of "escalation control" are dead wrong. Similarly misguided notions were circulating during the Cold War, suggesting that as conventional weapons improved they could replace nuclear weapons in a counterforce role and that had the United States launched a large-scale, partially effective conventional counterforce attack against the Soviet Union, the Soviets would have felt inhibited from responding with nuclear weapons because that would violate the rules of the game as defined by some western analysts and wishful thinkers. Fortunately, we never had to test that bizarre hypothesis in the intercontinental arena where the survival of the United States was at stake. At the very least, the selection of targets and the effectiveness of the attack, not the attacker's choice of weapons, are likely to dominate the equation. In some future regional conflict where nuclear weapons are involved, the stakes will be much less for the United States but could be considerable for the countries involved and any U.S. forces in the region. Perversely, the United States is likely to have more latitude to take risks in such situations, including relying on conventional weapons in situations where nuclear weapons have a clear edge in effectiveness. That, however, might be a tough sell to regional allies, although the politics could cut both ways depending on the circumstances. If the United States chooses not to use nuclear weapons in some particular situation, it should be for the following kinds of reasons:

- Conventional weapons are likely to be effective at whatever needs doing.
- The stakes are not high enough for the United States to warrant using *U.S.* nuclear weapons (an enemy might still decide the stakes are high enough to use *its* nuclear weapons if it could), particularly if there is still some possibility of preserving nuclear "abstinence" as a long-term rule of the game.

If anything, a "proportionality" test is a more appropriate criterion than escalation control. Escalation control was a dubious concept in most potential applications in the "old" world, because neither the

---

[10]Reed, op. cit., p. 8.

United States nor the Soviet Union could hope to gain such thorough dominance in situations that mattered that either could "win" an important victory without a major risk of an all-out nuclear war. Under these conditions, the "weaker" side actually controlled the rules of the game, and the combination of command and control procedures and limitations, mutual vulnerabilities, and massive forces impeded real control in any case. Ironically, in the post–Cold War world escalation control may actually have some meaning in quarrels where levels of power and political interest could be so asymmetric. However, it is not improved conventional capabilities that provide the control mechanism. The escalatory "club" that the United States always holds, and that any enemy should worry about, is its nuclear weapons, which it could use if conventional weapons prove inadequate militarily and if the stakes are very high or if retribution and political terror are U.S. aims. That tends to maintain some degree of coupling between U.S. conventional and nuclear capabilities. The coupling is relatively weak, as it should be, but it is there nevertheless, and that is important.

In summary, conventional weapons have the potential to perform most military tasks well enough that there should be little or no future U.S. military need for nuclear weapons *if* the United States fields adequate conventional forces, chooses its quarrels carefully, and manages conflicts in such a way that it is never in such a locally weak position that nuclear weapons are its only alternative. Unfortunately, the last point, in particular, is not entirely within U.S. control. The United States could still find itself in locally weak positions, such as it did during the early weeks of Desert Shield, perhaps faced by a nuclear-armed adversary. Then, the choices could become very painful if conventional capabilities have not been developed fully. The alternatives could be disengaging quickly or using nuclear weapons. Finally, no matter how good U.S. conventional capability is, it might not be good enough to prevent an enemy from using nuclear weapons. In that event, having nuclear weapons available either to destroy an enemy's military capability with higher confidence or to threaten devastating retaliation for a nuclear attack may have value even in the post–Cold War world.

Active Defenses

The final area of interest is active defense. Defense against nuclear weapons is making something of a comeback as the focus on the Cold War "balance of terror" moves more into the background and shifts to regional issues and emerging nuclear powers. It has even become a centerpiece of the Clinton administration's counterproliferation policy.[11] As suggested earlier, achieving stable regional nuclear balances may not be possible because of geography and offensive technology. Moreover, some nuclear actors may feel that they have nothing left to lose and may, therefore, be undeterred by threats of retaliation. Also, preemptive attacks against them may be ineffective. Against such enemies, effective defenses may be the only option.

Some elements of the problem are familiar; some have new wrinkles. Most of the new wrinkles are in the area of ballistic missile defense. Some favor the defense for a change:

- Defending against the kinds of relatively primitive medium-range ballistic missiles that many countries are currently acquiring is considerably easier technically than defending against ICBMs and SLBMs.
- The *technology* balance, at the moment, probably favors the defense.
- Although many more countries have ballistic missiles than have ballistic missile defenses and although ballistic missiles have actually been used in several theater conflicts, the sort of "offense dominance" that was a widely accepted pillar of the Cold War strategic balance of power has not emerged as an acceptable status quo to regional powers. If anything, the interest in defense against this class of missiles seems virtually universal.
- Several countries, including the United States, either already have or are actively developing complete theater ballistic missile defense systems or critical components for their own use, for sale on the international market, or both.

[11]John Lancaster, "Aspin Vows Military Efforts to Counter Arms Proliferation," *Washington Post*, December 8, 1993, p. A7.

- The kinds of systems being developed for theater defense would have no appreciable impact on the strategic offensive balance among the major nuclear powers if, say, the United States were to try to defend itself against a Russian attack.

All of this may account for the popularity of theater ballistic missile defense, at least in principle, even among some of those who have traditionally opposed ballistic missile defense for the United States. Moreover, as noted earlier, countries with hostile neighbors armed with ballistic missiles may have no choice but active defense due to the short warning times. Also, U.S. forces operating in such an environment may be excessively vulnerable without some kind of defense. As a result, pursuing theater ballistic missile defense is a relatively "no risk" venture for the United States, as long as the costs do not get out of hand.

On the other hand, the issue is by no means settled. Potential problems with theater ballistic missile defense include the following:

- It may not work. Even if the defense is effective initially, the offense might close the technology gap more rapidly than the defense can improve, again leaving the offense in a dominant position.
- Although the defense may have a *potential* technical advantage, the offense has an *actual* advantage in deployed systems at present.
- A truly effective defense may be unaffordable.

The United States and others should *focus on fielding operational systems with at least some useful capability as soon as possible* to try to take advantage of the temporary technical advantage that defenses may have over relatively crude Scud and No Dong–class ballistic missiles. Even that could be quite challenging, as the dismal performance of U.S. Patriots against Iraqi Scuds during the Gulf War demonstrated.[12] Moreover, even near-term systems may not come soon enough to solve some existing problems. For example, it is un-

---

[12]Tim Weiner, "Patriot Missile's Success in Gulf War Is a Myth, Israel Officials Say," *New York Times*, November 21, 1993, p. 8.

likely that *any* effective ballistic missile defense system could be deployed in time to help Japan deal with a potential nuclear threat from North Korea. That problem is likely to be resolved one way or the other before a defense could be deployed. Thus, the challenge for American diplomacy is to persuade Japan that the United States can protect it well enough from North Korea in the meantime that it need not take precipitous action itself, such as developing its own nuclear weapons.

Still, there are numerous possibilities for doing better with near-term surface and air-based systems, particularly with a bit of creative international cooperation and competition in selecting the right systems. Near-term deployment of theater ballistic missile systems, even systems with only limited capability, might alter the future shape of the arms balance in various theaters. It could offer an opportunity to "test" various traditional theories about the potential value of ballistic missile defenses (e.g., that deploying defenses might *not* lead to an offense-defense arms race that the offense is destined to win) and gain some actual "hands-on" experience operating such defenses before committing to more elaborate and expensive future systems. Failure would probably leave the participants no worse off (except for being a bit poorer) than they are likely to be if they forgo ballistic missile defense now. Success might reduce the chances of local nuclear conflicts and provide a means for dealing with at least one important aspect of the proliferation problem.

Despite the current enthusiasm for theater ballistic missile defense, even a relatively successful program will pose some difficult questions. One is balance. In the defensive arena, protection against the whole spectrum of potential nuclear delivery means—aircraft, cruise missiles, and unconventional means—is necessary to consider in establishing investment priorities. For the moment, aircraft and ballistic missiles are likely to be the delivery systems of choice. Since virtually all countries have some kinds of air defense, there is already some basic capability to defend against aircraft and a core system on which to build if improvements are necessary. In the long run, however, many countries with access to advanced technology are likely to opt for cruise missiles to replace aircraft and perhaps ballistic missiles in attacking surface targets. Defending against cruise missiles requires greatly improved air defense systems.

The point is that, although theater ballistic missile defense is the "flavor of the month," focusing on it to the exclusion of the broader defense picture could miss the mark. In times of scarce resources, determining how to balance investments among the different kinds of defenses is a particularly important and formidable analytical task. Moreover, against an adversary with more than a modest nuclear force, even a large, multifaceted defense might not be good enough, which makes the question of how much to invest in defenses more complicated still.

The balance issue extends beyond defenses. Les Aspin's December 1993 speech to the National Academy of Sciences emphasized a multifaceted approach to countering ballistic missiles, including locating them and destroying them on the ground as the United States and its allies tried to do in Iraq. During Desert Storm, the allies diverted large numbers of aircraft sorties and other resources to destroying Scuds with little success.[13] Given the overwhelming allied dominance of the war during the period when the Scud attacks were occurring, diverting resources to hunt Scuds really had very little effect on the allies' ability to prosecute the rest of the war. *In a future war, that story might be different.* A major decision that the United States will have to make is *how much it is worth investing in developing systems and devoting forces to trying to destroy mobile missiles on the ground, considering all of the other things those forces have to do and the chances of success against a competent opponent with nuclear weapons.* The jury is still out, but the answer will turn critically on whether hunting mobile missiles can be done tolerably well in the course of doing "business as usual" or if it is going to require large investments in new systems and large "opportunity costs" in terms of carrying out other missions.

Finally, revisiting the problem of strategic defense of the United States becomes unavoidable at some point. Unlike theater defenses

---

[13]Every book on the Gulf War contains a description of the Scud hunt. All agree that the effort mounted against them was enormous. While estimates of the overall effectiveness vary from low to nonexistent, by all accounts few Scuds were destroyed. Air power was particularly ineffective. Special operations forces may or may not have done slightly better. (See, for example, Rick Atkinson, *Crusade*, Boston: Houghton-Mifflin, 1993, p. 179; Lawrence Freedman and Efraim Karsh, *The Gulf Conflict: 1990–1991*, Princeton, N.J.: Princeton University Press, 1993, p. 309; and Douglas C. Waller, *Commandos*, New York: Simon and Schuster, 1994, p. 349.)

or U.S. conventional forces, strategic defenses obviously couple very strongly to U.S. and other countries' long-range nuclear offensive capabilities. These issues have been analyzed exhaustively—and exhaustingly—for decades and remain extremely contentious. The arguments almost always come down to what happens when defenses get good enough to upset the offensive balance that presumably helped the original nuclear powers navigate the shoal waters of the Cold War successfully.

Fortunately, it may be possible to bob and weave around the tougher aspects of this question for the moment in the post–Cold War world, dealing with some relatively benign, but important, things first and putting off the more difficult and contentious issues until the international smoke clears a little. First, the United States is helped by geography, and that is going to shape its defensive priorities. Only long-range aircraft or missiles can reach the United States from the homelands of most potential enemies. That helps a lot in the ballistic missile arena, because it means that an emerging opponent would need to develop either SS-25–class mobile ICBMs or SLBMs to have a serious operational capability. Otherwise, the United States would have too many offensive counters available. Even *that* sort of force operated by an emerging power is likely to be more vulnerable to attack than similar systems operated by the Russians.

The United States is, of course, still vulnerable to the ballistic missiles of the former Soviet Union and the other original nuclear powers. However, there is no compelling reason to upset the offensive balance with the Russians, which is enforced by mutual vulnerability, any time soon by deploying a ballistic missile defense of the United States. By the time such a defense might be technically feasible, the political climate might have improved to the point where the much-discussed "transition" problems would largely disappear. If not, the United States can either continue to live with its vulnerability to ballistic missiles or, particularly if ICBMs or SLBMs do proliferate, take the plunge and try to build a ballistic missile defense. In either case, *no decision is required now,* so the *United States should put ballistic missile defense near the bottom of its near-term priority list.*

Accidental launches, "mad major" attacks, or some sorts of catalytic attacks remain possibilities. Defending against such potential threats has engaged the attention of the strategic ballistic missile defense community for some time now. Ironically, now, when the former Soviet Union is in such turmoil and concerns remain about control of its nuclear weapons, is probably the time when such a capability might be of most use. However, a suitable defensive system is not yet available. By the time it could be, either much of the danger will have passed or the need will be much clearer.

Long-range aircraft are a more serious problem, but one that is more easily dealt with. Although very few countries have long-range bombers, virtually any nation, transnational group, or terrorist organization could get access to a commercial airliner or other sort of long-range aircraft. Moreover, aircraft are the ideal delivery system for first-generation fission bombs of the sort that new entrants to the nuclear club are most likely to acquire initially. Moreover, U.S. air defenses have been porous for decades. Thus, using aircraft might be particularly attractive for emerging nuclear powers or others to try to attack the United States with nuclear weapons.

The first steps toward solving this problem, or at least making it a less attractive option, are relatively easy. Since the advent of ICBMs, the United States has deemphasized air defense, seeing it as somewhat pointless when faced with a Soviet Union armed to the teeth with ballistic missiles. Still, the Defense Guidance has always cited a need to maintain "peacetime airspace sovereignty," which essentially means being able to detect, identify, and, if necessary, shoot down any individual aircraft trying to enter U.S. airspace. Now, the United States has never been able to actually do that, as drug smugglers and occasional defecting MiG pilots from Cuba demonstrate routinely. Still, the technical alternatives for surveillance systems that can detect and track aircraft-sized targets at any flight altitude are well understood, and the airborne interceptor force size and basing requirements necessary to allow fighters to identify visually any individual intruder and shoot it down if necessary have been worked out in study after study over the years. Moreover, the costs to develop real capability to deal with at least small numbers of intruders generally prove to be only slightly greater than the substantial costs the United States has incurred over the years to field and maintain a porous air defense system. Having an air defense system capable of detecting, identifying, and engaging a few intruders of any sort would not totally solve the problem of protecting the United States from aircraft carrying nuclear weapons, but it would do a lot while addressing other national needs at the same time.

Extending that kind of air defense capability to protect against at least ALCM/Tomahawk-class cruise missiles requires denser, higher-quality air defenses, but that problem, too, is relatively well understood, although a few contentious technical issues remain. Whether it is important enough to warrant the investment depends on how serious the threat becomes. Building a suitable warhead for a small, modern cruise missile, which is the kind of threat that could stress an air defense system, is probably not something that an emerging nuclear power could do the first time out. Even assuming rapid learning and maximum use of modern technology, a new nuclear power would probably have to develop at least a second-generation nuclear warhead for a modern cruise missile. That means that the United States has a little cushion in making a decision on deploying a cruise missile defense. On the other hand, ballistic missiles are almost certainly a longer-term threat from emerging nuclear powers than cruise missiles.

In summary, U.S. strategic defensive priorities ought to be defense against

- aircraft
- unconventional delivery
- cruise missiles
- ballistic missiles.

The first two are probably worth doing, although neither, particularly the second, is guaranteed to succeed. Defense against unconventional nuclear delivery, in particular, may not prove effective or affordable. The possibilities are poorly understood, although this is a "growth area" that is developing a cottage industry. The third and fourth may or may not prove to be justified, depending on how the world evolves. *None of these defenses may be totally effective even against very small attacks.* On the other hand, the nature of the nuclear future may be accepting some risk of a minor catastrophe in place of a smaller risk of Armageddon. On balance, that is a good trade.

Chapter Five

MOVING INTO THE FUTURE

The key for the United States in planning for the future in the nuclear arena is to *define a path* that begins with an *initial set of decisions* to establish a direction and then *identify key decision points along the way* where the direction can either be reinforced or altered according to how the world evolves. Defining such a process also provides some insurance against a de facto withering away of U.S. nuclear capability while no one is looking. Figure 1 illustrates the way the process might work and shows some of the key decision points. Tables 1–3 illustrate some representative U.S. nuclear force postures that might emerge depending on how things go.

The key points are the following:

- The critical set of initial decisions will shape the nuclear force for the foreseeable future. The focus is on platforms: submarines and bombers.
- Pivotal decisions along the way involve platforms—retiring SSBNs or bombers, say—rather than weapons. (These major decisions are indicated with more prominent arrows in Figure 1.) Decisions on weapons can be changed more easily. *Decisions affecting platforms should represent major "wake up calls" to reevaluate the world scene and overall U.S. strategy.*
- Note that *"withering away" involves more fundamental decisions* than either building up or maintaining the basic START II-like projected SSBN-bomber force.

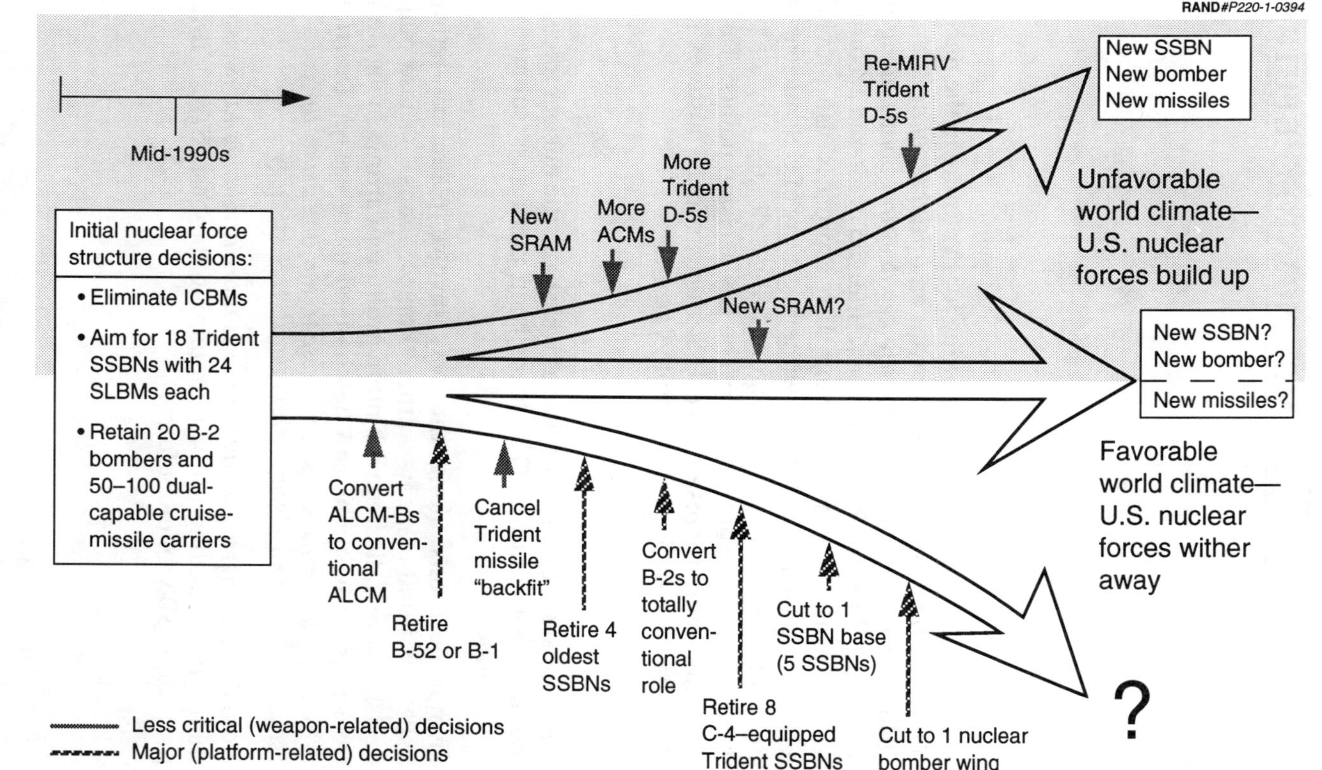

Figure 1—Key U.S. Nuclear Force Structure Decision Points as the World Evolves

Table 1

Notional Initial Target Nuclear Force Structure

Nuclear Platforms	Platforms	Number of Missiles/Bombs	Warheads
SSBNs	18	432[a]	1728
Bombers			
B-2	20	320[b]	320
B-52 or B-1 cruise-missile carrier	50–100	600–1400[c]	600–1400
Total		1352–2152	2648–3448

[a]Mix of C-4 and D-5 missiles, each with four warheads.

[b]All gravity bombs.

[c]Mix of ACMs and ALCM-Bs; total loadings depend on the bomber mix.

Table 2

Alternative Evolving Nuclear Force Structures—Building Back Up if the World Goes Sour

	Moderate Build Up			Serious Build Up—No START II		
Nuclear Platforms	Platforms	Number of Missiles/Bombs	Warheads	Platforms	Number of Missiles/Bombs	Warheads
SSBNs	18	432[a]	1728	18	432[b]	3456
Bombers						
B-2	20	320[c]	320	20–40	320–640[d]	320–640
B-52 or B-1 cruise-missile carrier	50–100	600–1400[e]	600–1400	100	1400–1600[f]	1400–1600
Total		1352–2152	2648–3448		2152–2672	5176–5696

[a]All D-5 missiles.

[b]Eight warheads per missile.

[c]Mix of half gravity bombs and half SRAMS (refurbished SRAM-As or new missiles).

[d]All SRAMs.

[e]Mix of ACMs and ALCM-Bs; total loadings depend on the bomber mix.

[f]All ACMs.

Table 3

Alternative Evolving Nuclear Force Structures—Withering Away by Design

	Initial Reductions			Moderate Reductions			Dramatic Reductions or Complete Elimination		
		Number of			Number of			Number of	
	Platforms	Missiles/ Bombs	Warheads	Platforms	Missiles/ Bombs	Warheads	Platforms	Missiles/ Bombs	Warheads
SSBNs	14	336	1344	10	240	960	0–5	0–120	0–480
Bombers									
B-2	20	320	320	20	320	320	0–20	0–320	0–320
B-52 or B-1 cruise-missile carrier	50	600–700	600–700	25	300–350	300–350	0–20	0–240	0–240
Total		1256–1356	2264–2364		860–910	1580–1630		0–680	0–1040

- The really major force structure decisions are going to occur in the early decades of the next century, when the United States will have to decide whether to initiate programs for a new SSBN and/or a new bomber as the existing systems approach the end of their useful lifetimes.

Budgets will, of course, be a major issue. The nuclear budget will be dominated by the SSBN force. Maintaining 18 SSBNs with a full complement of Trident D-5 missiles could cost from about $46B to over $60B, over roughly the next 15 years, depending on the life of the submarines.[1] Reducing the size of the SSBN force and the Trident D-5 missile buy could save billions of dollars.

The bomber force should be structured primarily for conventional operations, so while the "national cost" would remain relatively high as long as the United States operates a heavy bomber force, the charges to the "nuclear account" should be relatively modest. Thus, the major rationale for the bomber force has changed considerably since the beginning of the Cold War. Future bomber-related force-structure decisions should be largely determined in the requirements and budgetary requirements in the conventional arena. Only if the need for conventional bombers appears to be going away should the nuclear part of the equation become an important programmatic issue. Then, the United States would have to examine much more carefully the question of whether retaining a larger nuclear force with a substantial amount of built-in redundancy is worth the added cost of preserving the bomber force.

Whatever way the future unfolds, the sort of approach described here should, in conjunction with work going on in other military and specialized civilian high-technology areas, allow the United States to maintain an adequate industrial base to move in any direction. In particular, the United States should be able to retain its technological capability in at least the following potentially critical areas:

- Submarine design and construction
- Large airplane design

---

[1]Congressional Budget Office, op. cit., p. xiv. Costs are in 1994 dollars of budget authority.

- Ballistic- and cruise-missile design
- Stealth technology
- Guidance system and component development
- Mission planning
- Sensors
- Nuclear weapon technology.

The final throes of withering away, should that occur, are worth describing as well. The smaller forces shown in Table 3 reflect "quantum effects" rather than continuous reductions. At small force levels, the numbers result from retaining coherent units, such as one or two (or zero) wings of a particular class of bomber or keeping one or two (or no) Trident bases open. Intermediate numbers tend to be impractical operationally and are usually overly expensive. That is why platform decisions are so important.

All of the force structures presume basic operational changes as well as activity in other areas:

- Elimination of quick-response nuclear retaliation options and a move to highly adaptive planning, preferably as an integral part of routine theater planning
- Continued training and exercising with nuclear weapons
- Command and control modifications suitable for the post–Cold War environment
- A continuing, vigorous program to improve conventional weapons to eliminate the need for nuclear weapons for most, if not all, military missions.

These factors are actually much more important than the details of U.S. nuclear force structure in determining how well the United States will be able to cope with nuclear issues in the future.

Also, in a number of areas, key questions remain to be answered. These include the future of active defenses, the feasibility of protecting ourselves against clandestine delivery of nuclear weapons, and the possibilities for tracing the origins of nuclear attacks when the attacker takes pains to conceal his identity. These problems and possibilities will have to be evaluated continuously as other critical nuclear decisions are made. The result of this very dynamic process is likely to be a nuclear future that looks very different from the nuclear past, and being flexible enough to cope with that future is one of the most important national security issues that the United States faces.